A **Survival Guide** for
Working with
Bad Bosses

A Survival Guide for
Working with
Bad Bosses

Dealing with Bullies, Idiots, Back-Stabbers, and Other Managers from Hell

Gini Graham Scott, Ph.D.

⁄AMACOM

American Management Association

New York • Atlanta • Brussels • Chicago • Mexico City • San Francisco
Shanghai • Tokyo • Toronto • Washington, D.C.

Special discounts on bulk quantities of AMACOM books are
available to corporations, professional associations, and other
organizations. For details, contact Special Sales Department,
AMACOM, a division of American Management Association,
1601 Broadway, New York, NY 10019.
Tel.: 212-903-8316 Fax: 212-903-8083
E-mail: specialsls@amanet.org
Website: www.amacombooks.org/go/specialsales
To view all AMACOM titles go to: www.amacombooks.org

This publication is designed to provide accurate and authoritative
information in regard to the subject matter covered. It is sold with the
understanding that the publisher is not engaged in rendering legal,
accounting, or other professional service. If legal advice or other expert
assistance is required, the services of a competent professional person
should be sought.

Library of Congress Cataloging-in-Publication Data

Scott, Gini Graham.
    A survival guide for working with bad bosses : dealing with bullies, idiots,
back-stabbers, and other managers from hell / Gini Graham Scott.
        p.   cm.
    Includes index.
    ISBN-10: 0-8144-7298-2
    ISBN-13: 978-0-8144-7298-9
    1. Managing your boss.   2. Interpersonal relations.   3. Conflict management.
4. Interpersonal conflict.   5. Interpersonal communication.   I. Title.

HF5548.83.S365   2005
650.1'3—dc22

                                                                                2005015769

Printing number

10   9   8   7   6   5   4   3

Dedicated to:

All the bad bosses I and others
have had—without whom
this book wouldn't have been possible

Contents

Introduction

Virtually everyone has had some bad bosses over the course of their career, from the first job during or after high school to the present. In some cases, these bosses are aware they are "bad." In other cases, bosses may think they are great and don't have a clue what others think of them. You have hard-driving tyrants who measure success on the employee's productivity and don't give a fig if employees like them or are happy; for them the bottom line is all that matters. At the other extreme, bosses can be bad because they are so concerned with being liked, with being one of the gang, that they have problems with authority and control. When they spend all that time schmoozing with their employees, little gets done. They may be well-liked as a sympathetic, understanding friend, but that alone doesn't make a good boss.

So what is a "bad" boss? Essentially, any boss who is difficult and hard to deal with or who has trouble directing and guiding employees to effectively do the work can qualify as a bad boss. For example, such a boss might be incompetent, give unclear instructions, blame others, take undue credit, be high-strung and hyper, be disorganized, act like a power mad tyrant, or any combination of such characteristics. And in today's highly competitive, high-stress environment where a growing number of jobs are being outsourced and loyalty to a particular job or company is a thing of the past, the pressure and stresses that contribute to bad "bosshood" and difficult employer–employee relationships are more difficult than ever.

While the assessment of "badness" can be made more objectively by the boss's own boss, for employees, the subjective measure—what they think of the boss—is what counts. It's this latter approach we will take in this book, looking at what makes someone a bad boss and analyzing what can be done about it.

A Survival Guide to Working with Bad Bosses draws on real-life stories I have learned of in the course of consulting, conducting workshops and seminars, writing columns and books, and just talking to people about their experiences in the workplace. Each chapter uses a mix of problem-solving and conflict-resolution techniques, along with methods such as visualization, analytical reasoning, and intuitive assessment. In the end, the most important tool you have at your disposal is your common sense. You'll find that being straightforward and open where you can be, and otherwise playing your cards strategically and close to the vest, will produce the best results.

Since your livelihood depends in large part upon your relationship with your boss, you may find there are times when it's best to follow instructions and back off from stating exactly what you think. But on other occasions, you may do better to stand up for what you believe, even if it means possibly losing your job. An example might be if a bad boss asks you to do something illegal or unethical. Or perhaps a stealthier approach might be in order; there may be a way to expose your bad boss without getting stomped on yourself.

The best approach to use in a particular situation depends very much upon the circumstances. The ideal is to find a balanced solution that will allow for the greatest chance for success. You need to figure out when to follow the rules and when to bend or break them; when to be forceful and aggressive and when to back down; and when to act on your own and when to seek out alliances with other employees to negotiate with your boss together for the most satisfying solution.

However, while seeking that balance, it's important to recognize that no one approach or solution fits all. You have to adapt them not only to the situation, but also to your own style and personality, as well as that of your boss. And you have to consider if this is a problem that affects others or many others in the office or if it primarily affects you, which may make the difference in whether to seek a group or individual solution. Also, different principles, strategies, and tactics will work best for you at different times based on what's going on at the company, or even how your boss is feeling on a particular day.

Consider these chapters to be a series of recipes for better ways to deal with a buffet or smorgasbord of bad bosses. In keeping with this recipe approach, each chapter features the following ingredients:

⮑ An introductory paragraph highlighting the problem.

⮑ A short story or two about one or more people who faced this type of boss (with their identities, companies, and bosses concealed).

⮑ A quiz with a list of possible responses, so you can think about what you might do in a given situation. You can even use this as a game to discuss this issue with others and compare your responses.

⮑ A discussion of how these employees chose to respond to their bad boss or how they might respond.

⮑ A series of three or more take-aways to highlight the chapter's key points.

As you read about how other people have dealt with bad bosses, you might think about how you can apply these strategies yourself or use them to advise a friend or colleague with a bad boss.

I hope you enjoy this survival guide, and I hope it helps you to improve your situation at work. Read on and meet the many different breeds of bad bosses, those varied species of wildlife in the office zoo. Feel free to explore and visit these different boss species in any order, and as you do, think about what you can learn about how to deal with your boss. Think of yourself as a kind of "boss keeper": The more skilled you are, the higher your "boss keeper" score (your BKS for short), and the more tractable, pleasant, and helpful your boss will be.

If you have your own questions, feel free to visit my website at www.badbosses.net and send them to me.

Part I

Not Fit for Command

1 The No-Boss Boss

One of the most frustrating kinds of bad bosses is the boss who really isn't there: the "no-boss boss." This is the opposite of the overly aggressive, controlling, or micromanaging boss. It's the boss who manages by not managing; the leader who leads by not leading. This boss often does not make decisions and lets things ride until someone else has to make the decision. He's a boss who often does not know what is going on and depends on subordinates to know. In short, this boss may have the title, but in fact has left the ship rudderless or without a captain. As a result, management and leadership by default fall onto the employees. But this is not the same as a self-managed team, where team members have a clear idea of what they are doing, know who's in charge, understand the limits of their authority, and set their goals and tasks to get there. Instead, there is more of a sense of muddling along and filling in because the boss's lack of management has created a leadership vacuum.

How does a boss end up in or continue in this position? One common way is when a person with technical expertise gets promoted into management, yet is still making a good technical contribution. The person may even continue to be supported by upper-level management because of his contributions as a technical expert. As long as the boss has an assistant or other employees who can pick up the management/leadership slack, the situation can continue.

Yet, while some employees might welcome the freedom and autonomy of a boss who is missing in action, this situation often leaves employees frustrated and uncertain about what's going on. Additionally, some nonmanagerial employees taking on the management role might come to feel resentment and think they are underpaid, since they have in fact become the managers.

That's what happened to Corinne, who worked as an assistant to such a boss at a large company that created software for games. In her division, about 40 employees worked on software development. Her boss, Ben, reported to one of two company vice presidents. Though Corrine had been in her job for three years, she found it frustrating because Ben made no decisions. Corrine described Ben this way: "He's basically involved in his own little world, doing his own projects, creating his own programs. But he doesn't make any decisions or manage anything. If I or someone else goes to him with an idea, he'll say go with it. Or if there is some dissension or problem in the office, he'll put his head in the sand and keep working on his own thing, which involves programming and coding. I've mostly taken up the slack, and people come to me all the time to make decisions. Ben tells me to go ahead and do whatever I think is best. But it's really frustrating."

As an example, the company had a big meeting about a pending deal to acquire a large slot machine company. The other company's software division was much larger, with about 100 employees, so there was some question about who would end up running the division and whether there might be some company layoffs. But instead of talking about the pending deal, the meeting turned into a sales powwow about the new products the company would now be selling. Afterward, "everyone in our department went ballistic," Corrine recalls. "They were concerned about such things as, 'What's happening to my job?' and 'What'll happen to my 401(k)?' So about a dozen people came to me to find out, and we all went together to see Ben to find out what's going on. His answer was, 'I don't know.' He didn't even know what the meeting would be about before we went. I told him he would have to find some answers for everyone. But all he did was call up the VP, who's his supervisor, and tell him, 'You've got a problem. You have to talk to everyone and calm them down.' So essentially, he just dropped the problem in his supervisor's lap, and the VP called me to arrange for a meeting, which I did."

In most other cases, Ben simply rubber-stamped everyday decisions that Corrine made herself. Typically, his input would be, "That's fine. That's a good idea." And Corrine would go ahead and do it.

The office operated this way for three years, with Ben essentially taking a hands-off approach to management while Corrine filled in the gaps. Perhaps she should have been aware that such an arrangement might be the case when Ben first hired her. He had just been hired from another company, and he told Corrine her job would be to run the office. Although she didn't know a lot of the technical terms for the software products being developed, Ben left it to her to pick up whatever she needed to know on her own. He also left it largely up to her to figure out what her job should be and left her alone to do whatever it was, with little idea about or interest in what that might be. After Corrine was there for several months, Ben asked her to make a list of what she did. When she turned in a four-page list of job activities, he looked at her list in amazement, and said: "Damn. I didn't know you did all that. Keep up the good work." Then he went back to work on one of his projects.

While Ben had an open-door policy and invited Corrine or any employee to come to see him, the discussions had relatively little effect. According to Corrine, "He knows what we would all like: some more direction or guidance from him. But he doesn't do that. He can't make a decision and doesn't know what's going on himself."

So by default, people in the office came to Corrine for direction and she took over the management role. The situation dragged on for several years. Though Corrine tried several times to get out of that position and be promoted into management or work directly for the vice president, he didn't want to make any changes. Corrine got additional raises for staying where she was, so she was very well paid as an administrative assistant. The vice president told her, "You're the glue that holds everything together." So he wanted her to keep doing what she had been doing, rather than promoting her.

Despite feelings of frustration for herself and the other employees in the department, Corrine continued to accept the status quo and planned to ride out the upcoming merger. The vice president assured her she would still "fit in." Also, she suspected that Ben wouldn't make it through the merger, so another higher-level position might be in the cards for the future. For now, though, there was too much uncertainty to know. So Corrine decided to play a waiting game to see how it would "all shake out" over the next few months.

What Should Corrine Do?

In Corrine's place, what would you do and why? What do you think the outcomes of these different options would be? Here are some possibilities:

➲ Insist on getting a higher management title, not just more money, if you are going to be taking on a management role.

➲ Continue to make the decisions and don't worry about keeping Ben informed unless he asks, since he will generally rubber-stamp whatever you do.

➲ Reassure others in the department that you will be making most of the decisions, so they don't feel confused and frustrated.

➲ Don't be concerned about not knowing the technical details of the work because many managers are hired for their skill in managing people, not their technical knowledge.

➲ Since the vice president feels your role in keeping the department going is critical, be firm when you ask to be transferred into another position. He will realize he needs to do this, or you will leave.

➲ Keep doing what you are doing and wait for the merger, since you will probably be staying on and Ben will be gone. Then you can figure out what to do.

➲ Gather others from the department to join you and schedule a meeting with Ben to emphasize that you need him to provide more direction, decisions, and information, so the department will be more productive, and people will better understand and feel more committed to what they are doing.

In this case, you would probably do well to keep doing what you are doing, but learn to be more accepting so you feel comfortable with the situation. It seems clear that Ben really is not suited to or capable of being a good manager. He is a technical expert; this is what he likes to do and is good at, and he does not have the kind of people and managerial or leadership skills need for good management.

After a couple of years of this arrangement, it doesn't seem that it will be productive to talk to him about doing anything any differently. Ben probably can't or doesn't want to change, so there's no use trying. At the same time, the office seems to be thriving under your leadership, even though people are frustrated and confused by the lack of clarity. Thus, it might be good to clarify with others in the department what you are doing, so they expect to come to you for answers and decisions. It may be less necessary to include Ben in the loop on many of these decisions, since he doesn't seem to know or care about what is going on. Then you and everyone else might be less frustrated, and Ben may welcome the freedom from many day-to-day management activities. Perhaps you could tell him from time to time what you are doing, and point out that you thought this arrangement would help to relieve him of many responsibilities so he can focus on his projects. That way he at least will feel included and not pushed out. As you tell him about different decisions you are making and activities in the office, you can get a sense of how much he needs to know and either cut back on what you are telling him or tell him more.

As for the management title, you may have to let that go for the time being, since the vice president seems inclined to trust you to do the job but doesn't want to rock the boat. At the same time, you have been getting extra pay to compensate for your additional responsibilities. Once the merger is finalized, this may be the time to push for a formal promotion into a management position that reflects what you are actually doing. And there's no need to worry about knowing the technicalities of software development and coding, since you have 40 people in the department who know about those things. What they need from you are your management and leadership skills, not your knowledge about software.

In short, it would seem like a win-win situation for everyone if you were to continue taking over the management/leadership vacuum left by Ben's lack of interest in this role. Make it clearer to the other employees and yourself that this is what you are doing, and you will feel less frustrated and uncertain about what you are doing yourself. As long as upper management knows what is going on and rewards you for your efforts, you can probably count on a promotion sometime in the future.

Today's Take-Aways

- ☑ If there's a management vacuum, you can fill it yourself; after all, nature abhors a vacuum.
- ☑ If you have a boss who isn't acting like a boss, it may be because he really doesn't want to be a boss and would really rather just be a technical expert.
- ☑ If you're a better manager or leader than your boss, then go do it; in the long run, you will be recognized as a manager and a leader, too.
- ☑ If your boss is making no decisions, that is a decision to continue the status quo. If that's not what you want, seek to make the decision yourself so you are better able to get what you want.

2 The Pass-the-Buck Boss

Another type of bad boss is the "pass-the-buck" boss. This boss is in over his head but has one or more competent employees to take up the slack. The employees don't get the credit and often feel resentful. Yet they continue to protect the boss because they feel that's the best way to keep the organization running productively and later get good recommendations when they are ready to move on. Perhaps the more honest or ethical approach might be to protest and show up the boss's lack of organizational and task knowledge. But the co-dependent or facilitator approach may be more productive, at least in the short-term, for everyone in the organization. The employees who are knowledgeable get the work done, and they develop a good working relationship with one another.

That's the situation Bev faced as a graduate student, when she got her first paying job working as one of a half dozen assistant administrators in the university counseling department under Stan, the associate dean. The administrators' job was to act as academic advisers for the undergraduates; the dean's job was to coordinate the team, as well as help advise students with special problems, such as getting waivers and approvals.

However, as Bev complained, Stan wasn't up to the job; instead, he was an example of the "Peter Principle" in action. He had been promoted from being a counselor to managing a team of counselors and, as she described him, "He was very nervous and not confident about his ability to do the work." Among other things, Bev noted that "Stan wouldn't explain projects well, and when these assignments weren't done, he would harangue and berate people individually or publicly in staff meetings. He would lash out at the hapless staffer saying things like: 'You fouled this up big time,' 'What's wrong with you?' 'You should be smarter since you're a grad student.'" Stan also never took responsibility for not properly training and developing the people who worked for him. Thus, he frequently put down others for mistakes they made because he hadn't trained them properly, and he typically picked on the students who were cowed by his bluster and didn't challenge him. He even reduced some students to tears. Meanwhile, his colleagues got used to dealing with him and looked the other way when assistant counselors complained to them, telling the counselors, "Yeah, it's tough. But that's how it is."

The result of his behavior, according to Bev, was a dysfunctional staff response in which most of the graduate students tried to stay out of Stan's way as much as possible, said "Yes, sir" to whatever he asked, and took on his work in addition to their own. In fact, taking on his work became a team effort, as everyone picked up on the work Stan couldn't do, becoming a kind of self-managed team. As a result, the counselors felt much repressed resentment because Stan got the credit for their good work. Yet most of the student staff members didn't attempt to challenge him. They were just starting out in their careers, feared the consequences of confronting someone in a high-level power position, and wanted to do good work regardless because they were offering educational and counseling services.

When one student challenged Stan with a lawsuit and spent about two years fighting him, he fought back by making things even more difficult for her. For example, he frequently called her into his office to criticize her work and sometimes told her off and insulted her at meetings. Meanwhile, to smooth things over, Bev took on the role of facilitator and liaison between Stan and the students. Her sympathies, however, lay with the students, and they knew this. Bev would listen to the students' complaints, smooth out ruffled feathers, and reassure the students they did nothing wrong and to view whatever had happened as a learning experience.

Conversely, Stan would turn to Bev as well, both asking for advice and complaining about his difficulties with the students. For example, according to Bev, "Stan would ask me, 'What's going on? Why can't I get a good staff?' Then, I would try to reassure him about how everyone was trying." But when Stan tried to wheedle confidences from her to learn what was going on, she held back, not wanting to break her trust with the students.

This situation continued for the four years that Bev was there, and she felt that she and the others "kept his boat afloat." They did so, Bev thought, since the staff was made up of a group of over-achievers who were good managers themselves and found support among one another. In effect, they became their own managers, and Bev took on the role of a peacemaker between the students and Stan. Despite the feelings of resentment, anger, and frustration the students often felt, Bev helped to keep the system going. Looking back, she felt that she made the right choice for herself, though not for changing the system. While she said that the student who fought the boss made the most ethical choice and she admired her for it, she felt adapting to the situation worked best for her.

What Should Bev Have Done?

Is there anything Bev might have done differently, or did she make the best choice at the time? In Bev's place, what would you do and why? What do you think the outcomes of these different options would be? Here are some possibilities:

- ⮑ Stand up to Stan and challenge him when he is wrong. If enough people do this, it will force him to change or he may be fired.

- ⮑ Go along quietly like everyone else, and don't try to be a protector and facilitator; by doing so, you are only prolonging a bad-boss situation for everyone else.

- ⮑ Encourage the other team members to join you in a work slow-down for a day to show how important and underappreciated you all are. Then Stan will be forced to give you more recognition and treat you better.

- ⮑ Contact a senior administrator to explain that Stan is verbally abusing students at group meetings, which is reducing staff morale and productivity.

- ⮑ Take more of an advocacy role in promoting change, since Stan already trusts you as a facilitator and protector for the group.
- ⮑ Organize the students to confront Stan as a group since you are already helping them individually.
- ⮑ Continue to take on the facilitator/protector role since you understand the dynamics of the situation and everyone likes and trusts you as the liaison between Stan and the students.

In this case, Bev has probably made a good choice since she and the other students are just starting out. Getting the experience and a good recommendation is especially important at this stage in their careers. Also, they are working in a large educational institution in which firing anyone is difficult because of extensive protective procedures in place, and Stan had already performed successfully for many years as a counselor. His behavior—while abrasive, insulting, and disorganized—has not risen to the level of harassment or sexual abuse. The women as a group have developed a close, supportive bond as a team; they have been able to successfully perform the work and take over the management functions that Stan has not performed. Perhaps it is unfair that Stan should be getting the credit while the students have done the work, but this often occurs in an environment where new employees are learning how to do a job, particularly in a graduate school setting like this one. In this context, learning the job is especially important for future career development, and taking over this management role could be used as a selling point in applying for future positions.

Taking a confrontational approach to force the issue with Stan might actually be counterproductive, whether that involves challenging Stan at meetings, talking to other administrators about the problem, engaging in a work slowdown, or organizing a group confrontation. It would seem that the team-managed group that has evolved is an effective response to Stan's poor management skills since it both gets the work done and provides the employees with a source of group support and morale building. The relationship may be a codependent one, with a group of high-achieving, high-performing students supporting a less effective boss, but in this case it works. The job is an entryway to future jobs in the field, and taking on this extra responsibility can actually help the students individually in their job hunts. The situation would be different if the employees expected to stay in the organization and continue to rise within it. But here you have a relatively short-term arrangement where making the best of a difficult situation seems the way to go, especially since that will have favorable long-term results in applying for the next job.

Bev has not only been perceptive in evaluating the situation, but has created an even more effective role for herself in becoming a facilitator and protector for Stan, while helping to smooth out relationships in the group. So bravo to Bev for already making a relatively good, reasonable decision. Similarly, analyzing a situation so you understand the dynamics can help you in making your own choices about what to do, which might be adapting to the situation, rather than trying to change it, if that is the most sensible thing to do under the circumstances.

Today's Take-Aways

- ☑ Once you better understand the dynamics of a situation, you are on your way to resolving it.

- ☑ Just because someone's getting the credit now doesn't mean that you won't be able to take advantage of this credit later.

- ☑ Sometimes creating a self-managed team can be a good way to manage the situation, such as when you are facing a management vacuum.

- ☑ Try thinking about the different roles you can play to help resolve a problem between your boss and the work group; then when you choose the right role, you're on a roll.

3 Clueless but Connected

What if a boss has been put in charge by his family who own the business, but he is totally clueless about how to run things and doesn't know it? Often, because of the boss's family connections, employees may be afraid to clue the boss in, afraid the boss is untouchable and immune to any criticism because of family ties. But maybe that's not the case, and maybe the boss and family would really like to know what he doesn't know and how he could do a better job.

That's exactly what Randy experienced when he worked at a TV station as a news anchor and found himself with a new general manager, Will, soon dubbed the "idiot boss" by the employees. Will had gotten the job right after graduating from college; his parents owned the station. But it was clear early on that Will was in way over his head, and Randy and the other staffers reported that they "had no respect for him." As Randy explained: "He was not a people person and he had no knowledge of TV. So he would make irrational suggestions. He repeatedly came up with wacky ideas. We would carry them out and they wouldn't work." But no one dared to stand up to Will, fearing repercussions from his father.

Some of Will's ideas were more than wacky; they interfered with the way the station worked, impacting the bottom line. For example, he wanted to have more time checks when a TV crew was out in the field to see what people were doing, thinking this would make the team more efficient and accountable. But the amount of time required to do the time checks slowed the crews down. Even worse were his offbeat contest ideas to draw attention to the station. Since Will didn't understand how the TV newsgathering process worked, these ideas often disrupted the news operations. One contest around Thanksgiving challenged viewers to find the news truck and fill it up with pumpkins, with a prize for the person with the largest pumpkin that day. However, this created a very large problem because, as Randy explained, "the reporter can't be there gathering and reporting stories if people are bringing in pumpkins."

Unfortunately, Randy decided to fight fire with fire by playing his own practical joke on the station to show how dumb Will really was. He was sure Will would fall for the joke, since he didn't require sufficient fact-checking from the news staff. So Randy planted a phony story that a Neanderthal Village was discovered in one of the towns in the station's coverage area. He even used photos supposedly taken at this site. "Great!" Will thought. So rather than doing any checking at all, Will had the staff immediately go with the story, thinking this would be a major scoop. But the story soon unraveled when people called the local natural history museum and university archaeology department trying to find the site. Within days, Randy's role in creating the hoax was discovered and he was fired. Afterwards, the report about the incident in his personnel folder made it hard for him to find his next job in TV or radio, although he finally did. Thus, while the hoax may have helped to show up Will's shortcomings as a manager and demonstrate the dissatisfaction Randy and the other staffers felt, the most immediate result was the end of Randy's own job.

What Should Randy Have Done?

Rather than trying to point up Will's inexperience as a manager with a hoax, Randy might have done better with another approach to both express his frustration and let Will know what he didn't know. In Randy's place, what would you do and why? What do you think the outcomes of these different options would be? Here are some possibilities:

➲ Explain to Will when he has a stupid idea why it is stupid.

➲ Ask Will if you can meet with him to discuss station operations, so you can help him do a better job of running things.

➲ Organize others in the station and have a group meeting with Will to tell him what works and what doesn't.

➲ Send an anonymous letter to Will's father describing how his son has been messing up at the station and undermining operations and the bottom line.

➲ Organize a sick-out to protest Will's incompetence.

Here the basic strategy is to find some way to inform and educate Will as to what he is doing wrong and why, but in a gentle, understanding, and diplomatic way so he doesn't feel he is being attacked or is losing face. Rather than not respecting him, a first step is to inform him about the problem to see if that works. There is nothing wrong with a person not having knowledge and starting off with wrong-headed ideas. It's only wrong if the person puts up blocks to receiving knowledge and correcting uninformed ideas. Will's heart and enthusiasm to support the station seem to be in the right place; he just doesn't know what he doesn't know.

Thus, instead of making fun of him, try making him aware first, and if that works, the problem will be resolved. For example, depending on the circumstances, any number of efforts to enlighten Will might work, from informing him when particular ideas don't work to meeting with him individually or in a group to discuss the problem. Meeting with him as a group may be more comfortable, given his family connections. That's fine. There's more power and safety in groups, and if Will sees that a group of employees wants to educate him, that's more persuasive than going to him individually, and he is more likely to listen and take the input to heart.

But if Will is unwilling or unable to heed the advice, you can try step two: going above him to his father, preferably with other employees. It's important to let him know how badly his son is messing up as general manager, a fact which could affect the station's profitability. Emphasize the threat-to-profits argument, since that is usually a winner in family ownership situations and trumps the desire to protect an incompetent family member. But don't try the anonymous warning approach, which will often be ignored or trigger a search for the sender. This could backfire if it points back to you. Rather, look for some upfront way to get the message to the top person, such as sending a letter signed by most or all employees, or setting up a group meeting to discuss a serious problem. That approach is likely to lead to some top-down education and coaching, and that will likely solve the problem, too. What if it doesn't? Well, then you have an even more serious problem where you either have to learn to live with an incompetent boss, or dust off your resume and start looking for how to move on.

Today's Take-Aways

☑ If you've got a boss who's clueless, start by clueing him in. And if he's still clueless and so is his family, inform the family to show how this cluelessness is affecting the bottom line.

☑ People who don't know often don't know they don't know, so your task is to find a way to gently let them know what they don't know—or if they can't face it that they don't know, find another way to tell them what they need to know.

☑ Just like you give a hungry dog a bone, give a boss who's hungry for knowledge a clue. And if necessary, feed his family, too.

☑ Just as it's better to teach someone to fish than to give him a fish, it's better to teach a clueless boss how to find the answers himself, rather than just telling him. And sometimes it takes teaching the village, such as when the boss's family is clueless, too.

4

Scatterboss

While nobody wants a boss who hovers over them like a hawk and micromanages everything, the other extreme is the boss who doesn't follow up enough, or who gives an enthusiastic go-ahead but loses track of or interest in the project, resulting in unnecessary work for employees. This too-casual attitude can result in a last-minute flurry of activity to complete an assignment when a deadline suddenly looms and employees haven't been working on the right project. Worse, a continuing haphazard approach can leave employees confused, uncertain, and lacking direction. Even though they may like the boss personally, productivity and morale can be seriously damaged, and employees will start to flounder. While the boss may think she is empowering the employees, many of them may feel they need more clarity and guidance, and less empowerment. They would really like to know what their boss wants and learn of any changes in plans as soon as possible, so they can adjust what they are doing accordingly and cut down on unnecessary work and rushed deadlines.

That's what Leila experienced when she began working with Cynthia, who was in charge of several employees doing in-house communications for a medium-sized company that manufactured and marketed new and used boats and accessories for boat owners. The work ranged from creating brochures and other sales materials to taking photos of the boats and creating copy for a website. Plus, she sent occasional letters and newsletters to customers to check on their satisfaction with past purchases and let them know about new products and upcoming promotions. At one time, Cynthia had done the different projects herself, but then as the company expanded through acquisitions and adding more product lines, she hired one and then two, three, and four employees to do the work under her direction. Generally, different projects were assigned to different employees, so there was little need for teamwork. While everyone was friendly, people worked on their own in separate offices.

While Leila liked the work, she soon felt confused and demoralized because she wasn't always sure what Cynthia really liked or wanted her to do. For example, frequently Leila would show Cynthia a draft of an idea for a brochure, catalog sheet, or webpage, and Cynthia would gush about how much she liked the idea. So Leila would keep working on the idea, refining the design and getting it ready for a more formal review and production. But later, at the weekly staff meeting when Cynthia went over what the staff members were doing, Cynthia suddenly would tell Leila the designs weren't right or that the account executive for that product had changed her mind, so it was back to the drawing board to start over.

Another problem is that Cynthia would often change the deadline due date at the last scramble, resulting in a frenzied race to make the new deadline, such as when the proofs for an ad had to get to the printer a few weeks earlier than originally announced. And sometimes Cynthia wasn't very clear about what she wanted, such as when she dropped several different files of copy and graphics to be combined together into a single file format. Then, when Leila would ask Cynthia to explain, Cynthia was often in a rush, going to meetings with clients and vendors, and telling Leila to figure it out for herself. But many times Leila guessed wrong, which resulted in her having to make changes and sometimes missing deadlines. So Leila felt a growing sense of uncertainty, confusion, and frustration about what to do.

What Should Leila Do?

In Leila's place, what would you do and why? What do you think the outcomes of these different options would be? Here are some possibilities:

➲ Set up a meeting with Cynthia to explain that, although you appreciate her efforts to give you more responsibility and power, you need more direction and guidance.

➲ Find out from Cynthia the names of the account executives for whom you are doing work, so you can call them yourself to ask for more clarification.

➲ Ask Cynthia to give you a written list of when different projects are due, so you can better plan your work on different projects and meet the deadlines.

➲ Prepare a chart showing the projects you are working on, the due date, and what you are planning to do on each project so you can help Cynthia become more organized.

➲ Talk to the other employees to learn what problems they are having. Then set up a meeting with Cynthia to work out a way to create more organization in the office either by making Cynthia more organized or working together as a team to create better organization.

The major problem here is that Cynthia seems to be overwhelmed and disorganized in trying to coordinate a variety of projects for different account executives with varying deadlines. At times, these executives change what they want, making coordination even more difficult. Also, Cynthia has a problem directing and delegating. She doesn't provide enough information or keep the employees in the loop when she gets client input, and this results in Cynthia and others working on the wrong things. Another part of the problem is that until recently, Cynthia did the work herself and is not experienced in managing people, which is a very different skill. Perhaps a reason for her limited input is that Cynthia thinks that others know more than they do, so she doesn't give enough information or direction. Plus, she may think that leaving employees alone to do what they want at their own pace is a way to empower them and that employees like this independence. What she doesn't realize is that employees can't feel empowered unless they feel the power that comes from knowing and mastering a job, so she has to do more to organize the work and make sure employees know what to do.

Thus, the key is to help Cynthia become more organized in various ways. You and the other employees should take steps to educate her by making it clear that you need more information and direction from her to function more effectively. At the same time, you and the other employees can work on better organizing your own work and getting needed information from other sources if Cynthia seems too overwhelmed and busy. A good time to bring up these concerns might be at the weekly staff meetings, when Cynthia is going over what everyone is doing. For example, you might express the collective desire of everyone to have more information, including the contact information for clients and vendors, so they can check on how they are doing with these contacts directly. That way, they can make the necessary changes right away, rather than waiting for Cynthia to get this information and forward it on to them. In addition, this contact information could be used to clarify any initial questions about what to do after Cynthia has given out the assignments, should any staffer need to know more.

Additionally, you might explain to Cynthia how you would like to have a list showing when different projects are due, or better yet, a chart with a breakdown of what is needed to be done for each project. And if Cynthia needs help in developing this chart, you might offer your assistance. You certainly might meet with Cynthia individually to express your various concerns and work out a more organized way of doing her work. But where the problem affects a number of employees in a similar way, it is best, if possible, to have a group meeting. That way the problem can get resolved for everyone, and a group meeting cuts down on the time for individual meetings with similar results for all of the employees in the office.

Today's Take-Aways

- ☑ When your boss is disorganized and distracted, find ways to get her more organized and focused.
- ☑ If you aren't sure where to go, don't just plunge in, thinking you will find your way; instead, ask your boss to give you a map.
- ☑ If your boss is too busy to give you good directions, it may be time to make the map yourself.
- ☑ When your boss is a road block between you and others with needed information (such as clients and vendors), either ask your boss to take down that block or find a way to go around it to get the information you need.

5 Critically Clueless

Some bosses can have the best of intentions, yet be clueless about why their plans aren't working, and they don't want to hear why. They are in a state of denial. They don't want to admit that they are doing anything wrong, so they can continue doing what they feel comfortable doing. It's their way of protecting themselves from having to make changes they don't want to make. Even other managers or employees may not recognize the problem, since they are often getting their information from the boss. Or perhaps it may be the company policy. But what if it's wrong and you are certain that it is wrong? In some organizations, your input may be welcomed, but in others, not. Should you throw someone a life preserver to keep them from drowning, even when they don't want to be saved?

That's what happened to Henry when he got a job as a program developer for a social service agency after graduating with an M.A. in public administration. He came to the job with great enthusiasm, inspired by the agency's mission of helping families with children who were truants, runaways, or otherwise deemed incorrigible to stay out of the criminal justice system. Henry had always had a strong sense of wanting to help others and now he felt he could.

However, within a few days of beginning work for the agency, where he was tasked with writing up program plans and grant proposals, Henry detected a major problem in the way the agency was carrying out its mission. While the agency was located in a fancy new building in a large bustling suburban city, most of the clients with problem kids came from a few lower-income communities about 30 miles away. Typically, their parents struggled with part-time or temporary service or manufacturing jobs, such as working in a factory, gas station, or convenience store. When Henry went to the weekly meetings where his boss, Franklin, updated everyone on recent developments, handed out new case assignments, and led a discussion of current concerns, he soon learned that the agency was having trouble serving its clients. Why? Because as Franklin and the other staffers complained, the parents weren't regularly showing up with their kids for counseling meetings. When they did come, they weren't speaking up to discuss their problems, and if the counselors gave the parents advice on how to help their kids behave, the parents didn't follow it. Thus, as much as Franklin and the counselors wanted to help, they felt they were stymied by their uncooperative clients, who, in their eyes, didn't appreciate all the free services they were offering.

Henry soon came to realize the problem lay with his boss's policies. As he discovered after a few weeks on the job, his boss had his own way of running the agency to make it more convenient for himself and his staffers because they liked working in the downtown area of their large suburban city. But this approach was out of step with the needs of their clients. As Henry learned by asking a few questions about who the clients were and what they needed, many of these lower-income, struggling parents didn't have cars, so it was hard for them to get to the agency. Also, the parents and children weren't used to sitting down and talking to strangers in an office setting about their problems. They felt uncomfortable, even humiliated, at sitting in a stark white office facing one or two counselors across a desk. They were also suspicious that the counselors might be like welfare workers, school officials, or cops trying to get information from them that might expose them to penalties for doing something wrong.

The solution seemed so obvious: Why didn't the counselors go to meet the clients in their homes? And why wasn't the office located where the clients lived? Henry was amazed when Franklin told him the reason was that he and the social workers liked their slick new office building with its state-of-the-art computer equipment, and they didn't want to commute out to the boonies. Franklin didn't even seem to think that was a problem, noting that "it would be hard to find good staffers to work there." But clearly the problem was that the agency was catering to the needs of Henry's boss and the social workers instead of the needs of the clients it served. It was no wonder the program wasn't working, or that the clients weren't showing up or getting helped when they did.

But could Henry, as a brand new, just-out-of-grad-school employee do anything to remedy the problem, given that his boss and the staffers liked working where they were and expected the clients to adapt to their ideas what kind of treatment the clients needed? Should he even try to do something? And if so what?

What Should Henry Do?

In Henry's place, what would you do and why? What do you think the outcomes of these different options would be? Here are some possibilities:

- ⮑ Set up a meeting with Franklin and tell him why you think the program isn't working.

- ⮑ When someone complains about the difficulties of working with clients at a meeting, explain why you think it is so difficult; point out to Franklin why the agency needs to change its policy so the social workers can better respond to the clients' needs.

- ⮑ Write a memo to Franklin and the other staff members describing the problem with the current arrangement and suggest what the staff members should do differently, such as going to client's homes rather than expecting them to come to the office.

- ⮑ If Franklin doesn't want to make any changes, go above him by contacting the organizations funding the agency. Tell them what the problems are and how to resolve them, in the hopes these organizations will put pressure on Franklin to make the necessary changes.

- ⮑ Send an anonymous note to the funding agency complaining about why the agency is not really helping its clients and write it as if you are a disgruntled client.

➲ Suggest ways to help the clients travel to the agency and better serve them once they have arrived. For instance, you might recommend that the agency set up a shuttle service and that the counselors create a warmer, cozier area in the office for meeting with the clients.

➲ Drop occasional hints to your boss or co-workers in conversations about what they might do to better help the clients.

Unfortunately, this is a situation in which the logical solution may be obvious—bring the services to the clients and adapt them to the clients' needs—but it also cuts against the vested interests of the manager and his employees. While being a new employee on the job may help provide the necessary distance and detachment to see the problem, it doesn't bring with it the ability to solve the problem. In fact, being a new, lower-level employee like Henry makes it even harder, particularly since he is not a counselor dealing directly with clients but is developing new programs for the agency. As a result, should he approach Franklin or the other staffers directly, especially in a staff meeting, he is likely to make everyone defensive and protective of what they are already doing. The probable result would create a rift between Henry and the others, and perhaps lead to early termination and a poor recommendations for his next job. And any effort to appeal to outsiders, if they respond at all, can lead to even more turmoil. This might be great if you want a job as a political advocate or news investigator, exposing waste and incompetence in public agencies. But if your ultimate goal is to help others as a social service worker or program developer, becoming a whistleblower on your first job out of grad school is probably not the way to go. People in the field may be apt to label you a troublemaker, thus making future job-hunting more difficult.

So in a case like this, a good strategy might be just to observe initially, gain more information about the problem, and take notes to document what clients aren't showing up or following instructions. Then, you can gradually plant seeds of information as you get to know others in the organization. For example, you might make some comments in casual conversations with individual counselors about how they might make the clients more responsive, such as by taking a trip out to their homes or adding some fun decorations to their office to build rapport. But it's best to keep such comments informal and casual, so they are nonthreatening and appear more like positive suggestions than critical comments. In this situation, you can't make others change, but you can scatter the seeds of positive change. If they fall on fertile soil, such as a counselor who really would like to help, they will grow.

In short, in a situation where you are a new employee in a low-power position, think of yourself as a kind of gardener facing barren soil that needs fertilizer and water. The best you can do is plant some seeds and ask for some fertilizer and water, but you can only ask. You don't have the power to demand it, because if you do, you may not only be refused what you want, but you also might be forced to leave the garden.

Today's Take-Aways

☑   If you work with a boss and others who are clueless, they may not want to see the clues. You may do better if you reveal those clues to them slowly, so they may become more willing to open their eyes.

☑   Dropping clues to educate the clueless is a little like planting seeds to grow a garden; you need to take your time to give the person who is clueless time to respond to the clues.

☑   When you drop hints, you are more likely to get others to pick them up, whereas dropping bombs is more likely to lead to a big explosion.

☑   If people really don't want to see what is clearly in front of them, you may not be able to get them to open their eyes yourself; however, someone with more power and authority may be able to do so, if you let them see what is going on.

6 The Dishonest "Genius"

What happens when the top brass in an organization think your boss is a genius, but his underlings know better? They know the boss is deceptive and dishonest, yet they are demoralized and unorganized themselves, so they don't say anything. Such a situation is more likely to occur in a rigidly hierarchical organization, where the boss is the only one who has contact with higher management. In this case, employees have little power to press for change, particularly when the quality of the resulting work seems fine. To management, it seems the boss and his team are doing well. If only top management really knew that the boss was actually a liar and cheat who is not only taking credit for the employees' work, but is also on the take.

It may seem like you have few options to change what is going on. Or do you? Well, it all depends. Perhaps you might think of yourself as an enduring oak, while your boss is like a cloud, sometimes gray and threatening to storm, sometimes puffed up or wispy, and sometimes just speeding by. You're never sure what this cloud is going to do so you just try to stand firm and make the best of it, hoping to weather the storm.

That's what happened to Suzanne when she got a job for a major airline as a sales promotion writer. She felt a great sense of pride and liked the loyal, dedicated spirit of the employees working for the airline. But then she found it nearly impossible working for her boss, who had a team of dedicated, efficient women working for him, doing promotional copy on different projects.

As she described it, "Everyone in the company was so organized, efficient, and on time. But then Jacques would come roaring into the office around noon, and he would want everything done *tout de suite*. Though often, after you'd do it, he'd change his mind and want something else. It was so frustrating."

For example, Jacques once said he needed some promotional materials to support the airline's new business service to a new destination. He told Suzanne she had to get it done by Friday. But when she turned it in that day, he was furious, telling her that he wanted the materials to deal with leisure travel to the country's capital. Yet, he didn't acknowledge that this was a change from what he had originally asked her to do. "You could never be right," Suzanne explained, noting that her response — like that of the other writers working for him—was always to acquiesce, apologize for whatever he claimed was wrong, and do what he said he wanted now. The team members felt "stymied and trivialized," yet they continued to take it, not wanting to rock the boat and possibly lose their jobs in a great company. Moreover, the team members often put in extra hours to make changes and corrections to make up for Jacques's poor or inconsistent directions.

Why go along? Because Suzanne found that Jacques was the darling of the top managers and company owner. Jacques was the one who turned in the work for everyone in the department; he was the one who went to the meetings with the top brass. So management had no idea that Suzanne and the other employees all had complaints about his management style. Moreover, there was little chance the top managers would find out on their own, since the executive offices were all in the front of the building, while the promotional department was located in the far rear—which to Suzanne felt "like a hundred miles away."

Meanwhile, as Suzanne continued to go along to get along with Jacques' disorganized, on-a-whim, and take-the-credit style of management, she began to notice another major problem: Jacques seemed to be on the take or paying bribes to some of the vendors. As she discovered when she worked late for several nights each week, Jacques would meet with the department's main vendors after hours, when everyone else was normally gone. A few times, she saw money or envelopes change hands, which seemed suspicious.

Still, Suzanne said nothing, since she knew Jacques's bosses considered him a "creative genius," as other employees in the office told her. They had no idea that the employees in his department were unhappy that he was taking credit for others' work, or that he was on the take. Jacques was expert at making himself look like a star. Management didn't know what was happening below them. Moreover, since Jacques was careful never to meet with the members of his team as a group, but instead handed out the assignments on a one-on-one basis, there was no organized way for people in his department to bring up their complaints as a group. Is there anything any lower-level employee might be able to do in a similar situation with a disorganized and seemingly dishonest and deceptive boss?

What Should Suzanne Do?

In Suzanne's place, what would you do and why? What do you think the outcomes of these different options would be? Here are some possibilities:

⊃ Organize the other employees to meet with Jacques as a group to protest his lack of organization and find a way to improve communication and clarity in doing the work.

⊃ Write up notes after meetings with Jacques and send him a memo confirming your understanding of his instructions, and stating what you plan to do and by when.

⊃ Send an anonymous memo to the top executives in the front office to let them know that Jacques seems to be taking bribes or making payoffs to vendors.

⊃ Tell Jacques when you get your next assignment from him that you need him to be clearer in what he wants.

⊃ Stand up to Jacques when he tells you that you did the wrong assignment, and show him your written notes from your initial project meeting to show that he was wrong, not you.

⊃ Learn to accept the status quo, and look on this as a way to get a good reference for your next job.

While there are many things you might like to do in this situation, a good analogy would be a poker game, where the other player has all the good cards and knows it. You can't do much, and a power play or bluff is likely to cost you the game. A big problem here is the department's location far away from the central command, so you are in effect cut off from top management. And if the top executives are thinking of Jacques as their creative golden boy, a trait seemingly reflected in the work he turns in and in his charismatic performance at his regular meetings with management, you already have several strikes against you. So an appeal above Jacques' head is very risky and unlikely to get you anywhere. Because the other employees are not organized and seem inclined to do little more than let off stream through their complaints, trying to organize them may have a limited chance of success as well.

Thus, in a situation like this, the best strategy seems to be to make the best of a bad situation, particularly if you love the company but hate your boss. Think of the job as an endurance contest where you win the longer you can stay on, and this win will help you score and shine in the next competition. Meanwhile, do what you can to make your time at the company go more smoothly and comfortably.

For example, Suzanne might do what she can to clarify her assignments by writing down what she thinks she is being asked to do. She can then plot out what she intends to do and set deadlines for herself, and then send a memo to Jacques for a confirmation. This memo will also serve as documentation for a later discussion, if Jacques changes his mind. Still another possibility is to begin to cultivate a relationship with senior executives and managers in other departments. Eventually, you might find an opportunity to confide in them about what is going on. Another approach is to report what Jacques is doing to the human resources department, since kickbacks are the kind of thing they would investigate and, if true, would be Jacques' ticket out the door. But if you are new and Jacques has been with the company for a long time, this is a risky move early on, particularly if you are the lone wolf crying foul. Thus, it's better to first gain the support of others in the company who can back you up. No, this is not the optimal solution that might involve immediately showing up Jacques and exposing him for the disorganized, dishonest, deceptive boss that he is. But the risk of doing that is high, so unless you love the thrill of the high-risk career move, it's generally safer and surer to play your poor cards conservatively and keep the stakes from soaring up too high.

Today's Take-Aways

☑ As in poker, you need to know when to hold them or fold them, and in this case, folding may be the more sensible way to go.

☑ Don't think of the expression "If you can't beat 'em, join 'em" as another phrase for giving in. Sometimes joining 'em—or at least appearing to accept what's going on by remaining silent, since you don't want to do anything illegal yourself—sets you up for another win later down the road.

☑ When your boss acts like a flashy, jumpy hare, maybe it's better to move ahead like the quiet, steady turtle who ends up winning the race.

 That's Unfair!

7 On Overload

Generally, workers at the same level who receive similar pay expect to have about the same amount of work. But if they think a boss is giving them more or harder work than someone else, tensions can arise. They may feel the boss is being unfair and overly demanding, and resentment can build up. Even talking about the job can lead to escalating conflict when the boss's perception of the workload is different from the employee's and isn't willing to listen to the employee's point of view. This "my-way-or-the-highway" attitude can lead employees who feel they are unfairly treated and aren't heard to take their own corrective action to adjust what they perceive is unfair treatment, perhaps by taking more time for themselves when the boss isn't looking. They can also feel growing resentment toward employees in a similar position who are given a lighter workload for similar pay. Such dynamics can create a "haves vs. have nots" environment, where any employees who think they are on overload feel hostile toward those who don't have to work so hard. It's an environment that can easily erupt or lead to high turnover when the employees who feel overburdened burn out and leave.

That's what happened to Brett, who worked as a driver for a Meals on Wheels Program. Though he was hired by a top supervisor, he was assigned to a coordinator, Humberto, who was responsible for assigning the delivery routes. Besides delivering the meals, Brett was supposed to pack up the meals in the morning. In addition, if he wasn't able to make any deliveries—say, because no one was home—he was supposed to return the packages to the office and put away the food that could be used again. Within a few days, Brett began to feel that his route assignments were unfair compared to those of the other drivers for the organization. Though he received the same number of packages to deliver, he was assigned two different routes. One of his assigned routes went through the hills. The homes there were much farther apart, and Brett frequently had to drive through winding steep roads which slowed him down. Each of the hilly deliveries also took longer because Brett had a longer walk from where he parked the car in the street or driveway to the recipient's house. It was harder work, too, carrying the heavy food basket a long way to the person's house.

At first, Brett tried to complete his two routes within his normal shift time, but he repeatedly went over his scheduled time. He worked the extra hour or so without pay, figuring he was new on the job and learning the route. But when he spoke to other employees, he found that whether they had one or two routes, all of their routes were in the flatlands, where the houses were closer together and located on a grid of city blocks. The other employees could easily make their deliveries during their shift hours, sometimes even with extra time for themselves at the end.

Feeling the route assignment was unfair—since he was working longer hours and was working harder than the other drivers—Brett went to talk to his coordinator, Humberto. After Brett explained the problem, Humberto said he would check into the situation and would compare Brett's route with others in the organization. He agreed the routes were different from the other employees' routes and assured Brett that he would see to it he was treated fairly.

But over the next few weeks, Brett said, "Nothing changed. I still had the same two routes. Plus, Humberto also asked me to pick up food for the packages at the grocery, and he expected me to stay longer if I couldn't finish my routes in my regular shift. But he wasn't offering to pay me any more."

Again, Brett tried to talk to Humberto. But this time, instead of offering to check further into Brett's complaints, Humberto told Brett that the reason he couldn't finish the route in time was because Brett was too slow. Brett promised to try harder at becoming faster, but he felt the real reason for not completing his shift in the expected time was because one of his routes went through the hills, where delivery times were much longer. Moreover, he left the meeting feeling Humberto had given him even more to do, resulting in even more unpaid overtime.

"Humberto said I needed to be more of a team member and contribute more to the group, such as by measuring the bulk food into packages," Brett said. "But I'm the only one he's asked to do this packing. So I don't think that's fair. I feel like my boss is giving me all this extra work on top of my two harder routes, maybe because I'm new."

What Should Brett Do?

Is there anything Brett might have done differently? In Brett's place, what would you do and why? What do you think the outcomes of these different options would be? Here are some possibilities:

- ⮎ Do some research to find out how long others have taken on the route through the hills so you can compare your time with theirs.

- ⮎ Do a breakdown of how long it takes, on average, to complete each delivery in the hills compared with each delivery in the flatlands so you can show why your route in the hills is taking so much longer than these other deliveries.

- ⮎ Find out what work others are doing in addition to their delivery runs so you can compare the extra work you are doing with the other extra work, if any, that others are doing.

- ⮎ Send a detailed memo to Humberto based on your research on the extra time you are spending on the job and why. By doing this, you will be in a better position to argue your case, since Humberto isn't getting this information himself.

- ⮎ Tell Humberto you should be paid overtime for your extra hours of work. If he won't pay you, don't deliver the last meals on your route after the time is up.

- ⮎ Contact your union rep; you clearly aren't being treated fairly, so let your union rep argue your case for you.

You need to get more information before you can argue your case to show that you really are being forced to work overtime and are not just too slow in completing your routes and other tasks. You may well be overworked and underpaid, but you need to demonstrate this—first to Humberto, and then to anyone else, such as the union rep who may go to bat for you. Ideally, Humberto would gather this information as he initially agreed to do. But since he dropped the ball, perhaps because he likes things the way they are, you will have to take action and do some research yourself if you expect to see change.

Think of yourself as an investigator looking for the facts before you approach Humberto again to discuss the issue. To make the strongest case, you need some evidence that your workload is unfair. What should you look for? First, if someone in the past had the same routes that you have now, find out who the person is and how long it took him to make the deliveries. What did that person think? Did he feel similarly overworked and undervalued?

Secondly, since you have two routes but the same number of deliveries to make as everyone else, demonstrate how your workload is unfair because of the extra time it takes to complete your deliveries. Create a chart for your deliveries to show the miles between each house on the route and the average number of miles between all of the houses. Then, note the time for traveling to each of these houses and the average number of minutes for these deliveries. Finally, compare the times for the two routes so you can show how the terrain of the route increases the amount of time it takes for you—or anyone—to complete the route. You can then use this information to compare the average times on other routes. Perhaps you can recruit someone on another route to keep a similar record of his times for you, and maybe you can do something for that person in exchange.

Approach the extra work you are asked to do in the same way. Find out if other employees are doing anything in addition to their assigned routes. If so, maybe the extra work they do counterbalances the extra work you are doing. If not, you have more evidence with which to build your case.

Still another factor to consider is being new on the job. Find out from coworkers what is the norm for newcomers. In some cases, rookies are treated differently, and they may be given harder work as a test. Maybe you have the less choice routes now, but after a few months when you've proved yourself, you may find the work won't be so hard. Then again, maybe your boss is taking advantage of your good nature and is piling on extra work because he knows you'll do it.

In short, first get more information to determine if you are, in fact, on overload; if so, you'll need to demonstrate to your boss that this is the case. If talking to the boss yourself doesn't work, bring in some help, such as a grievance officer from your union or a legal representative who can seek to negotiate additional payment for your extra hours and work.

The information you gather can also help you decide if you want to remain on the job in the hopes that things will ease up later. Perhaps you will discover more efficient ways to make your deliveries in the hills or find that there are compensating factors for the longer routes, such as not having much traffic compared to snarled traffic in other parts of the city. Or maybe performing this research will lead you to discover that the problem is not that your boss is unfair, but rather that he is not good at keeping promises, following up, or training employees—maybe not the greatest boss in the world, but maybe not so bad as you thought, either.

Today's Take-Aways

- ☑ If you think you are overloaded with too much work, take a load off your mind by first finding out the facts about how overloaded you really are.

- ☑ If you can't get the information you need directly from your boss, try to find it out directly for yourself.

- ☑ Even if you know in your gut you're being treated unfairly with too much work, you still need to use your mind to find the facts to show why your treatment is unfair.

8

Only Good Enough to Train Others

When a boss asks you to train other people who are then advanced over you, it can undermine your morale and lead to resentment. The sense of being taken in, and taken advantage of, can become especially troublesome when you have been recruited with great fanfare and repeatedly told what a good job you're doing. The praise doesn't seem to jibe with the fact that the people you train get promoted while you remain in place. It's hard not to feel that your boss is playing favorites. In some cases, such unfair treatment can lead to complaints, or to a union or legal action, when the person who feels used gets angry enough.

That's what happened to Tamara when she got a job as an office assistant for a large insurance company. At the job interview with Henrietta, the woman who would be her supervisor, Tamara felt especially enthusiastic about the job because Henrietta told her how much she was impressed by her. She raved on and on about the great qualities that Tamara brought to the job, leading Tamara to feel Henrietta liked her very much. But then Henrietta concluded the interview by saying: "I'm so glad you are coming aboard. You're already one of my favorites, but I have to treat you like everyone else because I want to show I'm not playing favorites."

It was an odd comment, and when the relationship later turned rocky, Tamara wondered if this was Henrietta's way of getting the employees she hired each to think she was one of her favorites so she could get more work out of them. Tamara thought perhaps this was a power game Henrietta played to keep her employees in line and working harder.

Initially, Tamara did her job without complaint, thinking that this would help her get ahead. Her job for the next six months was primarily to work with the sales reps and provide them with support and follow-up. Among other things, she kept track of the different workers' compensation policies and loan policies that the reps sold by entering them into the computer and by filing and retrieving information from the company's extensive filing system. Plus, she answered the phones, and her feedback from Henrietta and the other employees was that she was especially good in this area.

But then Tamara began to notice a disconnect between what Henrietta said to her and what she was asked to do, leading her to wonder what was going on. As Tamara described it:

> *Henrietta started to hire and promote people over me, and she would tell me how fast they were, how quickly they picked up on what to do, and how high they would go in the company. But then she had me train them, and that didn't seem right. If I knew what to do well enough to train others, why not promote me?*
>
> *At the same time, while she had been so complimentary at first, she now told me I was too slow in completing the workers' compensation forms and that I wasn't good on the phones. So she gave me a bad performance appraisal. But it didn't make sense because I was still training other people who she then promoted over me. Meanwhile, the salespeople I spoke to over the phone never had any complaints.*

After a few weeks of this, concerned about what was happening, Tamara went to see Henrietta, but came away feeling Henrietta wasn't very forthcoming. "All she said by way of explaining the promotions and tough treatment of me is that she didn't want people to think she had picked me as her favorite." A few follow-up meetings with Henrietta over the next few months proved equally unsatisfying and left Tamara feeling puzzled and confused.

Finally, feeling Henrietta had been unfair, Tamara went to her union and filed a complaint. But when the union was ready to go after Henrietta for Tamara's seemingly unfair treatment and favoritism toward those she promoted, Tamara felt so discouraged she quit. She just wasn't up to a long, drawn-out battle.

What Should Tamara Have Done?

Is there anything Tamara might have done differently or did she make the best choice at the time? In Tamara's place, what would you do and why? What do you think the outcomes of these different options would be? Here are some possibilities:

- ➲ Keep a journal or log of the times when you feel Henrietta has been unfair so you can talk specifics, not just claim Henrietta is being especially tough on you.

- ➲ Set up a meeting to talk to Henrietta about what you find confusing and emphasize how you have been training the people that Henrietta has been promoting over you.

- ➲ Ask to meet with Henrietta to find out more specifically what she would like you to do, so you can do a better job and have a better shot at being promoted.

- ➲ Recognize that maybe Henrietta has a communication problem. It may appear that she is being unfair or playing favorites when she promotes the people you train over you, but maybe they really are better. After all, you are training them only in the basics, and there are many other aspects to the job.

- ➲ Don't wait for six months to complain to your union; bring them in right away to challenge Henrietta for what she has been doing.

- ➲ Stay the course and fight with the union on your side. You will be able to expose Henrietta's unfair treatment of you, especially since other employees feel you have been doing a good job.

- ➲ Notice what it is about the other people that Henrietta seems to have picked as her favorites and try to be more like them so you will truly become one of her favorites.

If you feel that you are the victim of unfair treatment or favoritism and that you are getting mixed messages, you should speak up more quickly, clearly, and diplomatically to clarify things with Henrietta. Documenting specifics in writing might help as well. For example, you might ask for more clarification on what exactly Henrietta feels you should be doing so you can do it better and faster. You might explain that you feel confused when Henrietta asks you to train other people who she later promotes without considering you for the promotion. Since you realize that just training someone else in the basics might not be the only consideration, find out what else Henrietta expects from you so you can be considered for promotion, too. You might also take notice of what the others who seem favored are doing to shine in Henrietta's eyes. Maybe they are really doing a bang-up job and deserve the promotion. The problem may not be so much that Henrietta is playing favorites, but rather that she gives that impression because she has a problem communicating to you what she wants or doesn't provide you with the necessary training and support so you can do a better job.

In short, seek to open up channels of communication with Henrietta so you have a better idea of what's going on and her reasons for promoting others and holding you back. Is it really that her favoritism towards others works against you, or is it more of a communication problem that is making you feel this way? If you still think Henrietta is unfairly playing favorites and holding you back, act quickly to inform the union and obtain their help. And if you think it's worth it to bring in the union to back you up, stay the course. After all, if you choose to fight and have an ally ready to support you, you have little reason to leave the battlefield suddenly in defeat without even trying to win.

Today's Take-Aways

☑ If you think a boss is unfairly asking you to train other people for promotion, determine what you can do to promote yourself. Find out what's really going on so you know what game to play.

☑ Sometimes it may appear as though your boss is playing favorites when the real problem is a breakdown in communication. In that case, take steps to repair the breach.

☑ When a boss seems to be playing favorites, the big question is whether the boss is playing fair. If so, try to find out why the boss has picked those favorites and see what you can do to become a favorite, too.

9 No Backup

A boss can also get bad marks from an employee for not providing backup against the mistaken comments or complaints of others. These others may not even be customers, but rather people who just observe the employee in action. Without such backup, the employee can feel discredited or disrespected when the boss doesn't provide the support the employee feels is deserved. The result can be lowered morale, as well as the employee not taking into consideration the input of outsiders, even when it would be more effective to do so, because he or she doesn't want to have to make the case for improvements to the boss. The employee goes along to get along and keep the job, although he doesn't do it as well and feels a lingering resentment because of the lack of support from the boss.

That's what happened to Sidney, a man in his twenties who worked as a shuttle van driver during the time between his discharge from the Army and heading off to college. His job on the morning shift was to pick up customers at an auto body and repair shop and drop them at home or another destination within a three-mile radius while they were getting their cars fixed for the day. The company's other driver picked up people from 2 p.m. to 6 p.m., usually to take them back to the shop. Sidney was a very friendly, helpful, affable guy who planned his route in such a way so that he could drop off his customers at their destinations and return for the next pickup as quickly and efficiently as possible. His boss, Tony, was in charge of getting the orders from customers over the phone and coordinating what the drivers did via the van radio.

I met Sidney while getting my car repaired, and his complaint to me was that Tony didn't back him up. This not only made him feel put down and disrespected, but also led him to unnecessarily adjust his driving so that it took longer to get customers to their destinations.

"People will call in and say I'm weaving in and out of traffic or going too fast," Sidney explained. "But what's happening is that people may see me in the fast lane and think I'm driving too fast, even though I'm driving within the speed limit. Or if I pass someone who's driving very slowly, they think that's weaving. So they see the phone number on the side of the van and call on their cell phone. I'll say I'm not doing that. But my boss is inclined to believe them, even though he should know me and know that I'm very responsible."

At first, Sidney tried to explain to Tony why the callers were wrong and how he was doing a good job by getting customers to their destinations quickly, without complaints. In fact, I found Sidney to be a very personable, concerned driver who engaged people in interesting conversations about their work and interests. But Tony didn't want to listen to any explanation and that bothered Sidney. "A boss should look out for his workers," Sidney said. "He should listen to what I have to say and support me, not some outsider on the street." Sidney complained that Tony treated his other employee this way, too: "He would rather keep the callers quiet and look for other workers if he has to than support his own workers."

Initially, Sidney tried to explain the callers' misperceptions to Tony, but since Tony didn't want to listen to him, he simply started driving more slowly, even though this was less efficient for the clients. "I just quit driving in the fast lane or the pass lane," he said. The result was that it took much longer to get customers to their destinations. Sidney felt demoralized, but he felt this change was the best way to keep his job. By contrast, when he had previously worked for a colonel in the Army doing office work and driving, the colonel would take his word over that of an occasional citizen with a gripe. Sidney felt that was the way a boss should be. "A boss should back up his people," he said.

What Should Sidney Do?

While Sidney found his own resolution by changing his driving based on the complaints, what else might he have done? In Sidney's place, what would you do and why? What do you think the outcomes of these different options would be? Here are some possibilities:

- ➲ Stand up to your boss more firmly. Explain how the callers are wrong, that your driving is fine, and that changing it will inconvenience paying customers since it will take you longer to get them to their destinations.

- ➲ Tell your boss that you feel that he should give you and the other employee more support and backup.

- ➲ Continue to adjust your driving to go more slowly and stay out of the passing lane so the callers will stop calling to complain, even though the service is slower for customers.

- ➲ Arrange a meeting between Tony, the other employee, and yourself so you can both ask for more backup and support together.

- ➲ Keep driving as fast as is safe and legal to provide the most efficient service to customers. Hope the problem with callers was just a passing incident and will go away.

In this case, Sidney has probably found the best solution, since others' impressions of his driving are so important, even if he is driving safely and within speed limits. At the same time, it doesn't seem that the customers are complaining if it takes him 5-20 minutes longer to get them to their destinations. Since these are one-time or only occasional customers getting their cars fixed, they may not be aware the trip is taking longer. Besides, Sidney has a way of cheering up the customers with friendly small talk, so the trip doesn't seem that long.

Thus, it would seem that Sidney's boss has probably made the right call in choosing to put the callers' complaints first, even if they are unjustified. But it also would seem that he has failed to make it clear to Sidney and his other employee why he has had to do so. This has left them feeling undervalued, disrespected, and resentful, yet afraid to say anything. They know that they are easily replaceable, and Sidney is aware that Tony has no qualms about hiring someone else.

Under these circumstances, it is probably best for you not to stand up to Tony to ask for more support, either individually or with the other driver. And continuing to speed and pass other cars might get you fired if callers continue to call in, since Tony has already spoken to you about the problem.

Your best alternative is the one Sidney has chosen: Adjust your driving and take more time to get customers to their destination. Perhaps you might also try to overlook Tony's lack of communication in not properly explaining his reasons for supporting the callers' perceptions.

Today's Take-Aways

☑ If your boss isn't giving you the backup you want, back up yourself and consider why your boss isn't supporting you.

☑ Sometimes the real problem isn't that your boss isn't giving you backup and support, but rather is failing to backup and support the reasons for *not* giving it.

☑ Standing up for more backup may not be the answer because you may leave your boss feeling unduly pressured.

☑ Sometimes, rather than trying to drive a hard bargain, it's better to adjust your driving to keep the peace.

10

No Excuses

Another kind of bad boss is totally insensitive and has no compassion when an employee has a serious problem, even a major injury or a death in the family. This boss's motto is, you must work when you are supposed to be on the job: no excuses, no exceptions. He is like the Army drill sergeant who feels that any kind of wavering will undermine discipline and performance, and anyone who doesn't adhere to the rules will be punished or fired. The people who stay are generally willing to quietly endure, yet morale and productivity can easily suffer, especially when an employee continues working in spite of an injury, family crisis, or other severe problem. Apart from quitting, is there anything that can be done?

Dominick came face to face with a "no excuses" boss when he worked at a maintenance job for an industrial cleaning company. After being laid off after several rounds of downsizing and unable to find another job in his high-tech field, Dominick felt lucky to land back on his feet—literally, in a job that required a lot of walking and lifting for eight hours a day. Although Dominick didn't particularly like the job, he desperately needed the money, so he kept at it, enduring the demands of his boss, Harold. Harold insisted that his employees arrive on time and work the full eight hours, except for specified breaks. That's what the dozen or so other employees did as they fanned out in groups of two to four to clean the offices in each building where the company had a contract.

After enduring this drill master treatment for about two months, Dominick experienced a crisis when one of his coworkers, Jimmy, who had become a good friend, discovered he had cancer and had an operation to remove the small tumor on his thigh. When Jimmy returned to work three weeks later, Harold simply asked him how he was, and then put him back into the same job doing heavy cleaning just like everyone else, even though Jimmy was clearly exhausted by the end of the day. The teams could have been restructured to permit Jimmy to do the lighter work, and he could have done some of the driving and office work while he fully recovered, but Harold never considered that. Nor did Jimmy ask, since he was afraid to confront Harold's insistence that if he was back at work, he should do his usual job.

Meanwhile, Dominick felt increasingly upset at seeing how Jimmy was treated, especially when Jimmy called in sick a couple of times because he was so worn out from the strenuous cleaning work. Like Dominick, Jimmy feared leaving the job due to tight economic conditions, and he was sure it would be even more difficult to get a new job, given his recent operation. Dominick felt tormented that the work was not only becoming harder and harder for Jimmy, but that it might even lead to the cancer coming back. He felt torn up inside seeing his friend suffer, felt guilty he hadn't done anything to help, and felt wracked with indecision about whether he should take any action that could jeopardize his own job. Yet he felt compelled to do something.

What Should Dominick Do?

In Dominick's place, what would you do and why? What do you think the outcomes of these different options would be? Here are some possibilities:

⊃ Stop feeling guilty and upset. Remind yourself that this is really Jimmy's problem, not yours, so you have no obligation to do anything.

➲   Since Harold isn't around much of the time, take over some of Jimmy's work and ask other employees to do the same to make things easier on Jimmy and help him recover.

➲   Talk to the other employees and tell Harold that you and the others would like to help Jimmy by taking over some of his work while he recovers.

➲   Talk to Jimmy and tell him he has to tell Harold that the work is undermining his health and might even cause the cancer to recur. Offer to come with him for backup.

➲   Find a time to talk to Harold and tell him of your concerns about Jimmy's health, since Jimmy is afraid to talk to him. Suggest that other employees can do the heavier work for him, and point out the company's liability if Jimmy's work leads to his cancer returning.

➲   Organize a group of employees to confront Harold and ask for better treatment for everyone—but especially for Jimmy.

➲   Speak to the company owner individually or as a group to explain how Harold has been treating everyone too harshly and hasn't been willing to make any allowances for Jimmy's weakened condition after returning from cancer surgery. Point out how the company could be sued if Jimmy's health deteriorates due to the job.

In this case, even though the most serious problem is Jimmy's, Harold's hard-hearted, insensitive behavior affects the whole workplace, making the work harder for everyone and undermining employee morale. In addition, for humanitarian reasons, Dominick should do something. While the work group can help by sharing Jimmy's burdens for awhile as he gets stronger, this is only a short-term solution. For a long-term solution, a meeting with Harold or even the company owner might be necessary. However, given that Harold is already insensitive, lacks compassion, and comes on like a tank in forcing employees to do what he wants with no exceptions for personal problems, talking to him individually probably won't work. And in a tight job market where you are doing relatively unskilled work, you have little individual leverage.

   Thus, a better strategy might be to get everyone together as a group to talk to Harold about giving Jimmy some slack, and showing

Harold how others in the work team can do some of Jimmy's harder work. Perhaps you could even point out the repercussions that might result if Harold continues to push Jimmy so hard before he is more fully healed, such as the company's liability if Jimmy's cancer recurs. And with everyone together as a group, this might be a time to ask Harold for more understanding in general if an employee has a special emergency, such as a serious illness or death in the family. One reason that this group approach might well work here is that Harold seems to be a boss who uses and appreciates power to rule the workforce. So confronting him as a group like an *ad hoc* union gives you more leverage to counter his power; if he sees he is outgunned, he is more likely to back down. But if you come to him individually in a position of weakness, he is more likely to see you as vulnerable and in no position to bargain so he has no reason to back down.

What if the show of force doesn't work? Well, you can always appeal to the head of the company. Here you may find a more understanding, compassionate person to hear your complaints of mistreatment, particularly when it comes from an organized group of employees expressing a similar complaint. Even if the owner isn't compassionate, he can understand the potential economic and liability issues that are at stake.

So yes, in this situation, you should definitely do something, but act in concert as a group so you have more power to force change since your boss isn't about to make any exceptions or allow any excuses for individual needs.

Today's Take-Aways

- ☑ If you've got a boss who's hard-hearted and tough like nails, take heart and do what you can to nail him as a group.

- ☑ If your boss treats everyone like a drill sergeant, it's time to change the drill—but understand that you can only do that as a group or by appealing above him to the higher in command.

- ☑ When someone else in your work team has a problem with the boss, remember that one day it could become your problem as well.

11

That's Perfect—Not!

A boss who is too much of a perfectionist and micromanager can drive you up the wall and right out the door. In some cases, perfection and precision is called for, such as in getting the numbers and data right. But when taken to extremes, this precise attention to detail can become excessive, resulting in frustration at the wasted time and effort as unnecessary work is done over, and over, and over again. This focus on getting a certain task absolutely—but unnecessarily—right can lead to the more important tasks not being done, resulting in bottom line losses for the company. Plus, there are extra costs for training new recruits after employees have transferred or quit. In short, being perfect to a fault can be a fault itself.

That's what Tanya experienced when she worked for a manufacturer of high-tech parts for industrial companies. She came to the job soon after graduating from college with an engineering degree and a flair for numbers and data. Her job was working as a manufacturing planner, which meant building and maintaining Excel spreadsheets to track the order status of hundreds of components for each product the company manufactured. The big problem was her boss, Edward, who never seemed to think the way she set up the spreadsheets was good enough. While Edward never questioned her numbers, he was an obsessive micromanager and repeatedly asked her to change the font size and the column sizing on her spreadsheets. He had gone through a dozen other subordinates in 20 years. Now Tanya was, as she put it, "unlucky 13." Sometimes Edward seemed to ask for changes just for the sake of having his employee make them. Tanya felt so frustrated by his picky requests for revisions that she decided to test him. As she described it in an e-mail to me:

> One day, Edward asked me to highlight the projects on the schedule in blue. After four changes, I decided to test him. I printed off the same document four times, with different shades of blue on them and the last one being the same shade as the first. I went through the first four, none of which was acceptable, because he didn't like the shade of blue I chose. Then, I went back to my desk, waited five minutes, and came back with another copy of the document in the original shade of blue, but I didn't tell him it was the same. Now he said it was "acceptable." But when I printed it out, Edward said he didn't like it after all and that I had ignored his "suggestions." So he deleted the whole document to force me to do it again from scratch—with still another formatting design and another shade of blue.

This is when Tanya decided her working conditions were unacceptable, and she put in for a transfer to another department. She felt that after nine months, she had endured enough, particularly since she averaged two hours a day creating documents for Edward and eight hours a day correcting them to meet his exact formatting standards, which seemed useless and unnecessary. Although normally employees had to wait one year to apply for a transfer, Tanya felt she had leverage since she knew how to enter the data; it would be difficult for someone else to perform this task without training. As a result, she spoke to Edward's boss, diplomatically explaining that she was seeking a transfer to expand her capabilities and contribute more to the company. Also, she explained that if she got a transfer, she would be glad to train a replacement. Otherwise, she wanted the company to pay a second person to work with her to help her with the extra work required in the position until she could transfer to another job. Tanya's request for transfer was granted.

Tanya trained Edward's new assistant—and a second one after that—but ironically, she was later assigned to be a project liaison between her new department and Edward's new assistant. Once again, her new job meant she worked in the same office with Edward, with his two new assistants on either side. Again Edward tried to give her "constructive suggestions" on how to format her reports to improve formatting for "readability" and to add in additional data he felt would make the reports more complete.

Tanya stood up to Edward, telling him:

> *If you have data you would like entered or changed, that's what your assistants are supposed to do. If you have calculations you'd like changed, take it up with the engineers. The format I use is standard for this kind of report. If you don't like one specific area, take it up with those who make those decisions. If you micromanage how a task is done, you are taking personal responsibility for the results. If you want all of these changes done and you want them to do it right, I have a simple solution— you will do all of this work yourself.*

In response, Edward complained to his assistants about Tanya's attitude and poor quality of work, claiming that's why she was transferred. Then he stormed off. When he returned, he demanded that Tanya personally make the changes he wanted. Tanya said, "Since I could never get it right when I worked for you, what makes you think you'd approve if I did it right now?" But he told her it was nearly 5 p.m. and he needed the report for a meeting at 8 a.m., so she better get started making the changes now, even if she had to work until 8 or 9 p.m. that night. Tanya waited until Edward left about 20 minutes later, then left herself without making any changes.

The next day, at the 8 a.m. meeting, the head engineer asked Edward for the project summary and Edward asked Tanya, "Where is it?" She said simply: "I didn't do it."

Edward looked at her in disbelief, exclaiming, "Excuse me?" to which Tanya replied, "You never did agree on a shade of blue, did you?"

Edward look mortified, and the meeting went on, since as Tanya expected, the status reports were only a minor presentation at the weekly meetings. What mattered more was that everything arrived on time and on budget, not whether or not the spreadsheets were pretty. After this, Edward never asked her to do anything on his spreadsheets again, so she was able to do a better job for the company. "I had to spend so much time on presentation that I didn't have the time to call suppliers who were late on orders or were having trouble meeting specifications," Tanya said. "Without Edward's nitpicking, I had the time to focus on the core of the job and did well in my new position. I had been unable to do well in my prior position because Edward's perfectionism had set me up for failure."

In short, after months of squabbling with Edward, both in her original position and as project liaison, Tanya finally found a public forum in which to squelch Edward's micromanaging of her work, and she went on to greater success in the company.

What Should Tanya Have Done?

While Tanya finally got Edward to stop his obsessive micromanagement of her work after her transfer, perhaps she could have resolved the problem much sooner. In Tanya's place, what would you do and why? What do you think the outcomes of these different options would be? Here are some possibilities:

➲ Ask Edward to give you written guidelines about exactly what he wants for formatting the reports. If he then claims you haven't done it correctly, show him these guidelines.

➲ Write up the guidelines that you believe Edward has given you to follow and get his approval. Then, if he claims you haven't done it correctly, show him these guidelines.

➲ Speak to Edward's supervisor early on about his excessive nitpicking and point out how these repeated changes for formatting are unnecessarily costing the company more than needed.

➲ Apply for a transfer much sooner, say after 2–3 months, and explain why you want to transfer.

➲ Agree to do one revision, and after that refuse to do any more, figuring that Edward will probably not fire you because he needs you too much.

➲ Bring up the formatting of reports in a meeting and explain how you feel it would be more productive to do the formatting in a standardized way, and suggest what that should be.

The basic problem here is that Edward is spending too much time on the format of the reports, when it is the content that really matters, and he is acting like an obsessive-compulsive in micromanaging and making repeated requests to redo the reports. In the end, Tanya ultimately began to stand up to him and he backed down, especially after a confrontation occurred in a meeting that revealed to higher-ups his obsessiveness for unnecessarily causing extra work. It showed that he was so focused on getting every last leaf on the tree right that he not only didn't see the forest, but was bumping into the trees. Tanya's main problem is that she didn't act quickly enough, either by refusing to do the unnecessary work or by speaking up at a meeting sooner. Had she done so, she might have avoided having to endure many more months of putting up with Edward's petty micromanaging.

Tanya might have also tried to get guidelines for writing early on, either by asking Edward to spell out exactly what he wanted in a memo or by writing such a memo herself and getting Edward to sign off on it. Or she might have sent Edward regular memos, letting him know her daily scheduled tasks and expected accomplishments so he was more reassured that she was doing what she understood he expected her to do. Then, he could make any corrections early on, before she did the work.

Tanya also should have recognized sooner that her knowledge gave her a certain amount of power in her position, given that she would have to spend some time training a successor. Since she was doing a complex job well, she couldn't easily be replaced. She could have asked for a transfer much sooner, citing her reasons, which would show why she felt Edward's actions were leading to much more work than necessary. Highlighting the negative impact his micromanaging was having on the bottom line is usually a good strategy with cost-conscious management. Additionally, she might have raised the problem with Edward earlier in a meeting, thus getting her conflict with Edward over formatting out into the open sooner. In turn, this public airing, done diplomatically, might have gained her some support from other higher-ups in the company who might have sided with her once they realized how Edward was creating unnecessary work, as well as friction with an employee who was doing good work.

If you face an unrelenting obsessive perfectionist who wants to micromanage everything and you are already doing a good job, try early on to stop the excessive management. One way is to keep the perfectionist well informed of what you are doing, such as through memos or copies of schedules, to reassure her that you are doing the work expected of you. Or if the requests to repeatedly redo work seem excessive, take a stand early on to clarify what is wanted, write it down, and keep it to show that you did what your boss originally requested. And if that doesn't work, be prepared to take your problem to your boss's supervisor, go public at a meeting, request an early transfer, refuse to work unpaid overtime, point up that you are already doing good work, and otherwise stand up for yourself. Then, assuming you are doing a good job and can't easily be replaced, your boss may well back down and reduce the micromanagement, as happened in Tanya's case when she finally stood up for herself.

Today's Take-Aways

☑ Be ready to stand up for yourself to keep from falling into an obsessive perfectionist's trap.

☑ If you are working for a perfectionist who expects too much, the perfect solution is to get the person to make it perfectly clear what she wants so you know exactly what to do.

☑ Sometimes a perfectionist can be a perfect idiot in demanding too much perfection. In that case, try making it perfectly clear to her boss or to other employees why this is so.

12

Promises, Promises

Another type of bad boss is one who makes promises that don't materialize. Broken promises can occur in any job setting. Bosses can make promises about raises, promotions, bonuses, commissions, extra vacation time, time off for overtime, and give any number of assurances that something will happen. Employees can easily overlook the occasional broken promise, but if pattern begins to evolve, they'll remember and feel devalued and unappreciated. That resentment can build over time, leading to acts of hostility: fudged activity reports, calling in sick to get promised time off, and more. When employees feel they can't trust the boss, they may become creative to get what they feel they were promised and what feels fair.

That's what happened to Ted, when he was hired as a housing and credit counselor. His job was to help first-time homeowners with low incomes or poor credit reports to obtain loans. The loans were guaranteed by the participating banks at being half a point below the current market rate, due to the backing of the federal government. When a loan was approved, Ted's organization received a 3% fee for processing the loan. Ted's job also included teaching classes to would-be borrowers on how to improve their credit scores or otherwise increase their chances of getting a loan, doing outreach to attract new clients to the organization's services, and writing grants.

Ted thought the job was a great opportunity, especially when his new boss, Sondra, promised him raises, a higher commission rate after a few months, and bonuses for good performance. But after some months, though Sondra kept praising him, the raises and bonuses and higher commissions didn't materialize. They weren't in the employment contract he signed, but Sondra said that was just an oversight. She assured him that he would get the promised raises and bonuses in the near future, once the organization's expected grant money for the year came through.

Over the next few months, Ted got numerous signs from Sondra that he was doing a good job. She took him with her to outreach meetings where they both spoke about the program. She brought him with her to the banks that were recruited to provide loans to clients. She asked him to teach additional classes. He also successfully set up and closed loans for a number of clients—as many as, or more than, the other employees.

But when Ted asked Sondra about the promised raises and promotion, she suddenly turned critical. She told him that he still needed more experience, had to improve in conducting the classes, and was taking too much time researching some of the loan applications, which meant it took longer to process them. Ted didn't think Sondra's assessment was accurate, especially since she was asking him to teach additional classes, and his rate of closing loans was as good as or better than that of others in the organization. But he backed off, not wanting to come on too strong, yet still hoping for a raise and promotion.

Then, an incident occurred that made Ted furious. He had been trying to get a home loan for Dick, an African-American man in his fifties who was active in a number of local political organizations. Dick was close to getting all of the information necessary for his paperwork, when Sondra learned that Dick served as director of a community organization that helped other organizations obtain grants. Unaware that Ted was already working with Dick as a client, she called him, pleading her case for grants, and very quickly undermined Ted's own home loan efforts. What happened? According to Ted, "Dick had come to our organization for help in getting his own house, and he wanted to see how the program worked for him as an individual before he was ready to help her. When she called him, it made him wonder about the financial stability of the organization and its ability to get him his loan. Plus, it made me feel stupid that

Sondra contacted him and didn't know I was working with him. Here I was supposed to be knowledgeable in helping him get his loan, and then my boss calls him like I didn't exist."

Ted not only felt Sondra had failed to keep her promises to him, but he also felt betrayed by her for going to Dick on her own. Plus, he also wondered whether he got the full commissions that were due to him in the past, or whether he would get the commissions that would be due to him from deals he had already set up that would close in the future.

What Should Ted Do?

Is there anything Ted might have done differently or could do now? In Ted's place, what would you do and why? What do you think the outcomes of these different options would be? Here are some possibilities:

- ⮑ Tell Sondra how her actions undermined your ability to close the loan with Dick.

- ⮑ Make up a list of all the loans you have closed and all the commission earnings you should get from these loans.

- ⮑ After you are hired, ask Sondra for a memo of understanding about what commissions you are supposed to get. If she doesn't write it up, write up your own understanding of what you are entitled to and give it to her.

- ⮑ Ask Sondra to give you a performance review after you have worked there a month so you know more clearly how you are doing and what you might do better.

- ⮑ Contact a union representative to speak to Sondra on your behalf about the commissions, raises, bonuses and promotion she promised for good performance, and provide your rep with documentation to show what you have done.

- ⮑ Use the incident with Dick as an opportunity to ask Sondra to keep her past promises about raises, bonuses and a promotion. However, be prepared to be fired and file a wrongful termination suit if she doesn't come through.

In this case, it would probably be good to determine early on just what Sondra was actually promising and what was more of a general hope of acting if the organization received the grant money for which it had applied. It may be that Sondra's promises about bonuses, raises and promotions were conditional ones, contingent upon the organization's earnings, as well as your own performance. As a result, if the organization hasn't gotten the expected grants, it may be that Sondra really didn't make a promise she hasn't met. Rather, she has not been clear in communicating exactly what she was promising and under what conditions. Thus, asking for a memo of understanding or writing it up yourself when you first start working there would be a good way to go.

Commissions, however, are a different matter entirely. They should be based on the loans you are able to close and not on the possibility of grant money received later on. If you feel that you are not getting the commissions you are entitled to, you definitely should speak to Sondra and get a clear agreement on what your commission rate is and what it is based on. If you haven't done this already, ask to set up a meeting to clarify these arrangements or write up a memo about your understandings and failed expectations, without being accusatory.

This meeting might also be the right time to bring up the problem of Sondra's contacting your client, but again, don't be accusatory. Instead, explain how you were working with this client and helping him obtain a loan. Tell her that her call to your client to inquire about grant money has made him uncertain about the organization's solvency and, as a result, reluctant to continue seeking his own loan. Once Sondra understands the situation, she might be able to help clear up the misunderstanding. Perhaps she can call your client directly to apologize for the inappropriate interference, and you can then go back to your relationship with him as it was before.

Requesting a performance review after being in the organization for a few weeks or a month or two might also help, showing your interest in doing a good job and improving your performance. Again, there could be a communication gap in how you interpret Sondra's requests to teach more classes or accompany her to outreach meetings and how she sees these requests. Perhaps she sees these activities as opportunities for you to continue learning and improve, but she isn't giving you any feedback to help you teach the classes better or conduct the outreach meetings on your own. So while you might think Sondra is giving you signs that you are doing well, maybe she sees these as additional learning opportunities.

In short, if you feel a lack of trust in your boss because of unkept promises, you need to have a frank, nonaccusatory discussion about what you and your boss believe these promises to be so you can see if you are on the same page. Before you consider anything more confrontational, such as calling in a union representative, both of you need to get your cards on the table so you can see what your hands actually are. You may find that you are closer together than you thought, or that you misunderstood what your boss was actually promising. Whatever the case, this is the time to get a full understanding—in writing—of what you can expect as to promotions, raises, bonuses, commissions (if applicable), or anything else that you feel you have been promised.

Today's Take-Aways

- ☑ If you think your boss isn't keeping his promises, first clarify what those promises actually are.
- ☑ Sometimes something may sound like a promise, but it's really a conditional offer to do something and not a promise at all.
- ☑ Even though a verbal promise can become a legal agreement when you rely on it, you and your boss may remember the promise differently, so either get it in writing or write it down yourself and send a copy of your understanding to the boss.

13 No Trust

Sometimes trust between employee and employer can break down not because of broken promises, but because a boss is devious and secretive, and sets employees against each other in a Darwinist make-or-break style of running the office. When the employees discover what the boss is doing, resentment builds, and morale and productivity suffer. Employees no longer trust the boss with any information or concerns and may even work against him if they can. Meanwhile, the boss is often unaware of what the employees are feeling or doing because they are acting individually or in concert behind his back. The reason for all this stealth is that when a great power divide exists, employees are afraid to bring their problem to anyone higher up in the organization. The net result is that the untrustworthy boss continues to rule over a group of unhappy employees who express their anger and frustration to each other and sometimes take subtle action against the boss to show their resentment.

That's the situation Rod encountered when he got a post-doctoral research job in a biology lab at a large university. His job, like that of many post-docs, was to conduct independent research projects under the guidance of Dr. Harris, a noted professor and lab director who was to be his mentor and would ultimately get the main credit for any successful research results. About a dozen people worked in the lab, and unbeknownst to each other, Rod and Susan, another researcher, were assigned to do the same research. Instead of collaborating and sharing information on the same project, Rod and Susan were actually in competition with each other. Dr. Harris, however, didn't tell them about this competition. It was one of many ways that he kept information from the lab researchers, though Rod found this deception especially devastating when he discovered it. He felt his whole research project was based on false information, and it shaped his relationship with his boss for the rest of his three-year research assignment.

Rod learned of the deception after three months on the job at the weekly meeting of everyone in the lab. At this meeting, Susan, who had been at the lab for four months, described the research she had been doing and her preliminary findings. Her project sounded exactly like what he had been doing, so he mentioned this to Susan right after the meeting. Then, as Rod and Susan discussed their parallel projects, they realized for the first time that they were working on identical assignments. Immediately, they both felt frustrated and angry that they had been misled to believe they were doing original, independent research, when in fact, their work was duplicative.

Yet, despite their anger, neither said anything to Dr. Harris. Instead, Rod and Susan continued to do what they were doing, though now with little enthusiasm and motivation. As Rod explained:

> I felt I had just wasted about three months of my time doing exactly the same research project as someone else. But Susan and I didn't say anything to complain because we were so unequal in power to Dr. Harris. He was this big-name, powerful professor and research director, and we were both working in our first research jobs. We felt he wouldn't give a damn what we thought. So we just continued on, though we each did a somewhat different experiment to set up one as a control test. Ultimately, the experiment didn't work anyway, which in a way was a vindication for the way he treated us.

While both Rod and Susan continued to work at the lab, the incident changed their relationship with Dr. Harris irrevocably. According to Rod, "It undermined our trust. We became closed and secretive, and we didn't go to the professor anymore for advice or input, though he was supposed to be our mentor. We only spoke to him when he came around and asked questions or gave instructions. We spoke to others in the lab about what happened and discovered they shared similar feelings about the way Dr. Harris had treated them."

Over time, Dr. Harris's treatment had a negative effect on the lab generally because people started to look for other positions. Those who remained became secretive about their research results until the research was completed, rather than sharing during the process, which was the norm in the field. "We all closed down to the guy, and he began to lose talent because no one trusted him," Rod said. "Also, since no one trusted him, we didn't tell him about our results until we had written them up because we felt he might give this information to others in the lab or outside it. And if he did that, the researcher could lose any credit for doing the research." Although the researchers understood that Dr. Harris would get the overall credit for their research, being recognized as part of a successful research project was a major type of reward in the field. "If you give out the information before you write a paper about your results, another person could jump on the bandwagon or get published before you," Rod explained. "But once you submit your paper, your credit for the work is secure."

In this case, it didn't matter, since the research did not produce any useful results. But Dr. Harris's treatment led Rod and others in the lab to feel paranoid, as well as powerless to do anything about their treatment. In fact, Rod felt that remaining silent was the best way to get along after he learned that it did little good to confront Dr. Harris about anything. For example, after Rod and a dozen other researchers asked Dr. Harris about getting new equipment, Dr. Harris not only turned down the request, but badmouthed the researchers to other research directors at the lab. And when one woman stood up to him, seeking to be part of a claim for intellectual patent rights, screaming matches ensued, and she ultimately had no support for her research and didn't get her degree. By contrast, the researchers who were quiet and went along with whatever Dr. Harris wanted got good recommendations. "So the unwritten message," Rod said, "was to keep your mouth shut to do better at the lab, and that's what most everyone did."

What Should Rod Do?

Is there anything Rod might have done differently or do should he have such a boss in the future? In Rod's place, what would you do and why? What do you think the outcomes of these different options would be? Here are some possibilities:

- ➲ Chill out. There is no reason to feel upset or paranoid; this is just the way things are in your field. Get over it.

- ➲ Do a completely different research project, since Dr. Harris isn't paying attention to what you are doing and someone else is already doing what you were assigned to do.

- ➲ Talk to the other researchers who feel similarly powerless, and join together to formally protest to Dr. Harris about the way he is treating all of you since he can't risk having everyone leave.

- ➲ Continue doing what you are doing by quietly sharing research information with Susan and not rocking the boat. After all, you have little power and need a good reference for your next job.

In this case, as a new employee with little power, a very powerful boss, and a tradition of little concern for the feelings of employees in this field of work, it is probably best to do what Rod ended up doing. He quietly collaborated with Susan and they adapted their experiments to turn one into a control case so they could compare results under two conditions. At the same time, it might help to be more accepting of traditions and culture of the field in order to feel less angry, frustrated, and paranoid. Since there is little likelihood of changing these everyday norms of behavior, having an attitude of detachment might be the best way to cope with the situation. Rather than complaining and sharing gripes with others, which probably only reinforces your feelings of anger and frustration, focus instead on what you do like about the job.

While it might have been ideal to be collaborate with Susan on the research from the get-go, you might consider the independent projects a way of providing further confirmation if the two experiments show the same results. This is actually the reason that many science experiments are duplicative, and why experiments are often done again and again to provide such confirmation. Maybe Dr. Harris should have told you that both of you were doing the same thing so you could share information from the start. But he might have kept you in the dark because he felt it would give the experiment's results more integrity if you didn't share. In any event, such secrecy combined with a tradition of independent researchers conducting duplicative experiments is part of the culture of the field. Consider that it comes with the territory; if you want to stay in the field, you will learn to live with it. Since you have little power in the lab, it is probably best not to rock the boat. Instead, learn what you can from the experience and get a good recommendation for your next job in the field.

Today's Take-Aways

☑ The old expression "When in Rome, do as the Romans do," sometimes applies in the workplace as well. When you are starting off in a new field, remind yourself that it's in your best interest to adjust to and accept the norms if you want to stay in the field.

☑ Sometimes when you close down to a boss you don't trust, that opens up new possibilities for what you can do quietly behind closed doors.

☑ When you can't talk to a boss you don't trust, you can find comfort and support in talking to others who feel the same way. Just don't let the boss hear it and you'll be fine.

14

You're Great, But . . .

A boss who doesn't fully show appreciation for his employees can cause feelings of frustration, lowered self-esteem, and poor motivation. But equally as demoralizing can be "backhanded compliments," that is, when a boss continually combines praise with negative put-downs. On the one hand, the boss is seemingly complimenting an employee for a good performance, but then comes the follow-up punch—a judgmental statement about something, maybe even several things, the employee is doing wrong. When you are confronted with a positive and a negative, the negative will often seem stronger. You feel like you are being buttered up only to be put down; given a reward only to be set up to get a punishment. This can end up making you feel bad or angry toward your boss.

That's what David experienced when he worked as a technician for a telecommunications company. As he described it, his boss, Herb, was an expert in backhanded compliments. It was as if his boss had steeped himself in the management literature about the importance of praising the troops to get them to perform better. Herb worked very hard to give compliments daily, but there was always a kicker. "The only problem was that he couldn't say anything nice without leading up to it with one or more negative statements," David said. Or alternatively, he would give the compliment first, and then follow up with one or more put-downs.

For example, one time Herb walked up to David's desk and told him: "David, you may screw up around here a lot, but I just want you to know how much I appreciate that you never call in sick and are always here on time." Another time, he told David: "That was a great job you did in helping that customer today. I just wish you could be on target more often." On yet another occasion, he said: "David, thanks so much for working overtime so you could diagnose and fix that customer's problem in one day. That was really good, since you had to leave early a few times this week."

David found such comments confusing and demoralizing be-cause, as he put it, "when he walks away, you wonder if that was a reprimand or a compliment." In turn, these so-called compliments left David, like other technicians subjected to such comments, feel-ing angry and resentful. They never said anything to Herb, but griped among themselves and sometimes took out their frustration by giv-ing themselves their own small rewards, such as extra time for a break because they felt unappreciated. In effect, Herb's backhanded compliments ended up backfiring because his put-down left a stronger impression than the compliment itself.

What Should David Do?

Should David continue to take it or not? In David's place, what would you do and why? What do you think the outcomes of these different options would be? Here are some possibilities:

- ⊃ Remind yourself that this is Herb's personal quirk so you don't take the put-down personally and feel better by focusing on the compliment instead.

- ⊃ Respond to Herb's two-sided compliments with a joking com-ment that shows you know what he is doing, such as saying something like: "Hey, are you complimenting me for the job I did on my most recent assignment, or is that a put-down?"

- ⊃ Have a private meeting with Herb to let him know that his com-pliments combined with put-downs leave you feeling upset. Ask him if he could compliment you without the put-downs, or con-versely, offer constructive criticism without a trumped-up com-pliment.

⮑   Bring up the issue at a staff meeting. Tell Herb how you and
    others have been bothered by his style of giving compliments,
    and hope that once you have broken the silence, others will ex-
    press their similar feelings.

⮑   Organize a small group of employees who feel similarly and have
    a private meeting with Herb to share your feelings about these
    backhanded compliments. Indicate that you are speaking for
    others in the office who feel the same way. Ask him to give
    everyone compliments if he feels they deserve them without
    adding in the negative assessments, or vice versa.

Depending on the circumstances, any number of these approaches—
individually or in combination—might work. Just don't suffer in silence because the double-edged compliments are causing feelings of
resentment and lowered self-esteem and are interfering with productivity. It would seem that Herb is actually well-meaning in trying
to compliment and motivate people but doesn't know how to separate any criticisms of worker performance from the compliments. Or
perhaps Herb thinks that using the compliment to inspire might help
make any criticisms go down better, like putting medicine in a sugar
drink so it tastes better and is easier to drink. When it comes to
workplace criticisms, it is generally best to keep them separate from
praise in order for the feedback to have maximum effect. If Herb
knew how his compliments were actually having a negative impact,
he might want to change himself in order to achieve a more positive
result.

    To this end, some informal joking about his compliment style
might be a good way to start. With this approach, you point up what
Herb is doing in a humorous, nonthreatening way, where kidding
makes the serious message go down more easily—a little like what
Herb has been doing in sugarcoating his criticisms with compliments. If that doesn't work, another step might be having a private
meeting with Herb to let him know your feelings. Keep the conversation focused on the matter at hand. Tell Herb how you would prefer
he show his appreciation when he wants to compliment you. In
other words, gently and diplomatically describe your experience in a
neutral, nonaccusatory way. Couch your message so that Herb sees
you are seeking an improved relationship with him, not trying to
cast blame.

If Herb seems accepting of your message—and he might well be, since he seems to genuinely want to show appreciation—you could let him know that other employees feel the same way. That acknowledgment could open the door for other employees to discuss their feelings with Herb, too. However, avoid turning this expression of feelings into a big encounter at a staff meeting, as doing so could end up making Herb feel embarrassed and defensive. This is a situation where gentle diplomacy might be the best approach, and it might give Herb a chance to show how much he really does appreciate you and others, while saving the negative comments on what you could do better for another time.

Today's Take-Aways

- ☑ If you're getting mixed messages, it may be that the person giving them isn't aware of it, and it's time to point out the mix-up.
- ☑ One way to stop backhanded compliments is to lob them back.
- ☑ When compliments come with a "but," don't take "but" for an answer.
- ☑ When your boss seemingly means well, but seems to be, well, mean, it's time to show what these words mean to you so he can change.

Part III

Power Players

Just for Sport

You can feel like a football when you have a boss who likes to play with the underlings, setting up roadblocks and embarrassing or humiliating employees for amusement. Sometimes this boss will pit coworkers against one another, creating unnecessary rivalries. It's like the boss is a coach who enjoys moving players around the field or benching them on a whim to show who is in control.

That's what happened to Gloria, when she worked as a researcher at a consumer products company where there were a half dozen senior vice-presidents in charge of various product lines. Her job was to report to two of the senior vice presidents, Judith and Max, who shared responsibility for one of the product lines but hated each other so much, they didn't even speak to each other directly. Instead, they communicated only through their secretaries. Unfortunately, Gloria's job was to work for both of them, and the budget for her position was split right down the middle. In theory, she worked half of the time for each of them, though in practice, she spent most of her time working directly with Judith.

Soon after she was hired, Gloria found herself in play between the two rivals. Judith called Gloria into her office to assign her to a new project that involved researching the positioning for a new product. Gloria enthusiastically dug in, and about a week later, sent Judith the finished report, along with a memo requesting her approval to release the completed report to the rest of the company. Judith sent a memo back to tell her she also needed to get Max's approval before releasing the report. Gloria went to his office with the report and Judith's memo, thinking this just a routine request, and unaware of the rivalry between the two.

At once, Max exploded, angrily yelling at her: "How could you have done this project without my input?" When he finally calmed down, he said he would have to review the report himself. When he did, he came back to Gloria with what to her seemed like minor, cosmetic changes, as if these were his way of putting his own footprints on the report before signing off on it.

Afterward, Gloria felt she had been set up, and she later learned that Judith set up such encounters from time to time between the employees and Max to flex her power and get Max riled up as a kind of fun sport. Additionally, Gloria soon found herself attending the department's weekly round-robin meetings at which all of the employees would take turns giving reports on what they were doing to keep all the vice presidents informed of the latest developments. As they did, Judith's style was to take pot shots at all the presenters by asking nitpicky questions and pointing up things they had done wrong to put them down in front of the entire department. Sometimes she even made comments about people's clothing or hair. But no one sought to challenge her out of fear of further escalating the confrontation. Also, despite her bullying and game-playing, Judith did have a good sense of what would sell in the consumer marketplace, and her division continually wracked up good sales.

Though Gloria liked doing the research itself, she didn't want to continue to be a punching bag. So what should Gloria do about dealing with Judith and navigating through the rivalry that Judith had with Max?

What Should Gloria Do?

In Gloria's place, what would you do and why? What do you think the outcomes of these different options would be? Here are some possibilities:

➲   Check with Max before doing any new projects to see if he expects to have any input.

⮕ Ask Judith before starting a new project whether you should show this to Max first, and then send Judith a memo confirming your understanding that Max should or should not see this. This way, Judith will be exposed if she plays the keep-Max-out-of-the-loop game.

⮕ Write up memos or e-mails to Judith to confirm what you are doing, ostensibly to show your understanding of the project, but also to provide you with documentation in case you need to challenge Judith.

⮕ Diplomatically respond to any of Judith's attacks on you at a meeting by pointing out that you were only following her directions, and refer to a memo you have written to show this.

⮕ Talk individually to other employees who have been victims of Judith's games or attacks. Suggest that they follow your strategy of clarifying when Max should be involved in a project and of standing up to Judith's attacks at meetings.

Judith has clearly become a master at playing these games, since no one is calling a foul play yet. The way to defeat her at her own game is by mastering and changing the rules, as well as invoking some stealthy tactics to undermine her play. Commonly, a boss who is engaging in underhanded game playing to put down others is acting out of a sense of inferiority, so she constantly has to best others or reaffirm being the puppetmaster. The key to overcoming this, unless you want to acquiesce to get along, is to make it clear that you won't be sucked into the games. When you do assert yourself, however, don't provoke a one-on-one confrontation, which might get you fired for insubordination. Also, be careful not to reveal what the boss is doing at a general meeting, as this might create an embarrassing confrontation for everyone.

Instead, when you feel your boss is using games as a power play, try to stop the game by keeping a record of the various plays. Also, write your own memos to show what you understand is the object of an assignment, how you should do it, and what approvals are needed. Such a straightforward documented response will make the boss less likely to use you in any games she might be playing. Then, for any public confrontations and put-downs, counter by explaining what you understood and provide documentation to show that you did what you understood. Where possible, share your strategies with other coworkers who are also victims in the power play so they can respond similarly. Once your boss sees that the games are no longer having the desired effect, she is likely to lose interest.

The advantage of this stealth approach is that your boss can stop the game playing without losing face. She can simply leave the playing field quietly, and you've achieved the result you wanted: The end of the game.

Today's Take-Aways

☑   If your boss is playing games with you and others, come up with some plays to end the game.

☑   As they say in sports, the best defense is a good offense; likewise, in the office, think of writing memos like keeping score and your first line of offense.

☑   If someone tries to use you like a football in an office power play, don't go where you are kicked; instead, see yourself as one of the players.

Turning Yeses into No's

Working with a boss who only wants to hear yeses can be annoying, but it can become an even more serious problem when the boss wants you to say "yes" to something that's clearly wrong, even criminal. Certainly, there are many downsides for the boss who only wants yeses, since she doesn't learn important information about what's really going on. The result can be a state of denial when things are going badly, with the boss operating in a kind of bubble. This can be just as disastrous for a company as for a political administration that screens out negative information. This hear-no-evil approach may feel good for awhile, but then grim reality sets in, and the company is usually worse for having not dealt with the problem early on. Unfortunately, some bosses prefer to operate in this situation where nobody contradicts them and nobody gives them bad news. Meanwhile, employees who maintain the state of denial are encouraged and rewarded for their loyalty in supporting the boss, even if she is wrong, while others who point out any problems are ignored, squelched, or even fired. They are like whistleblowers the boss doesn't want to hear, or chirping canaries the boss doesn't want to know about. He or she would rather shoot the messenger than hear bad news.

So what do you do when you have a boss who only wants yeses and doesn't want to listen to any nos?

Victor encountered this problem when he worked for a fast food franchise company. His boss, Jarvis, frequently wanted Victor to do things that went against company policy, such as cutting down the size of the portions to increase profits, and placing his own messages in local ads without first getting them approved by company headquarters. Jarvis said he didn't want to get caught up in the company bureaucracy and wanted a more streamlined approach.

At first, Victor, like the four other employees at the branch, went along with Jarvis's requests. One reason that Victor did this is that when he questioned Jarvis about anything, his boss became defensive. "He didn't want anyone to challenge him, and he liked to do things his own way," Victor said. So Victor backed down and quietly did what Jarvis said, though privately he questioned the ethics of what Jarvis asked him to do.

But matters came to a head when one day some money was discovered missing from the cash register at the end of the day. Jarvis felt he knew who had taken it: Perry, one of the other employees, was recovering from a drug addiction and had had conflicts with Jarvis in the past. However, all four employees had used the cash register during the day, and the money could have been missing due to a mistake in giving change. Nevertheless, Jarvis felt so certain Perry had stolen the money that he asked Victor to be a witness for him.

"He said he knew who stole the money and wanted a witness so he could put the thief in jail." At first, Victor resisted by telling Jarvis, "I don't remember seeing anything." Then Jarvis insisted: "But he stole the money. I know he did." Victor firmly refused, saying he wouldn't do it. And Victor stood his ground, even when Jarvis challenged him, suggesting, "Well, maybe you're involved in this, too."

That was the last day Victor worked for Jarvis. He just walked away feeling humiliated, without even taking his pay for the week. He just didn't want to deal with the situation anymore.

What Should Victor Have Done?

While Victor finally stood up to Jarvis, it took place in the middle of an ugly incident that left him losing nearly a week's pay. Perhaps Victor could have acted sooner or differently to achieve a better outcome. In Victor's place, what would you do and why? What do you think the outcomes of these different options would be? Here are some possibilities:

- ⮑ As much as you can, quietly ignore Jarvis' orders that contradict company policy, such as cutting down on portion sizes.
- ⮑ Send an anonymous note to company headquarters to let them know that Jarvis is deliberately ignoring company policy to the detriment of customers.
- ⮑ Talk to the other employees about the different ways in which Jarvis is asking you to violate company policy or lie about another employee. Confront him as a group to demand honesty.
- ⮑ Tell Jarvis that not only do you refuse to lie for him, but also that you don't feel comfortable about possibly sending an innocent man to jail. Reinforce your position by informing you will contact the police yourself to tell them what happened.
- ⮑ Tell Jarvis that you don't feel comfortable making up a story for him and go back to work. If Jarvis fires you, insist on being paid.
- ⮑ Agree to lie for Jarvis, but if the police contact you, tell them the truth. Jarvis deserves it if he's caught in a lie.
- ⮑ Support Jarvis's story, since Perry probably did steal the money and you need to keep your job.
- ⮑ Talk to Perry about Jarvis's accusations to learn Perry's side of the story firsthand and decide what to do based on whether you think Perry is guilty or innocent.

When you're a low-level employee like Victor in a company where the boss is in control of day-to-day operations, you may not be able to do much about how the boss chooses to run the business, even if it contradicts company policy. This is a fairly gray area, where operational decisions like the size of the portions and pricing are more in the nature of business decisions, and Jarvis's choice to ignore or resist company policies might be considered more of a contractual issue. So setting your opinions against your boss's demands is likely to be viewed as inappropriate and, as a result, you will fail. It also may be hard to get a group of other low-level employees worked up enough about such an issue to attempt a group challenge. Thus, it may be necessary to continue to go along, i.e., to say "yes" to your boss's rules and policies, even if you don't agree with them. This is probably your best option if you want to keep the job and leave with a good recommendation.

However, if Jarvis's efforts to undercut company policy are egregious enough to undermine the company's reputation or possibly endanger the customers' health (such as using shorter than recommended cooking times to save time), then it might be appropriate to inform higher-ups in the company about what's going on, since Jarvis is unwilling to listen to you. One way is to send an anonymous letter or make an anonymous phone call to describe what has happened. But be prepared for the possibility that your name may eventually come out. It is always a tricky situation when you decide to be a whistleblower, however meritorious your effort to expose what an employer is doing wrong. But if the boss is unwilling to listen to any criticism, blowing the whistle may be the only way to go, whether you choose to stay at the company or leave.

The case of lying to implicate another employee in a crime is a totally different situation, however. Don't do it! First off, it's bald-faced lie that could potentially put an innocent person in jail. You really don't know if Perry is guilty just because Jarvis strongly suspects him. Worse, it could get you charged with a felony for giving false testimony in a criminal case. So here Victor was right to stand up to Jarvis. He just didn't stand up strongly enough to get Jarvis to back down or to leave the job with full pay.

For example, as soon as Jarvis asked you to commit a criminal act, you could have refused and explained that this would subject both of you to criminal penalties for bearing false witness. Then, if Jarvis insisted, you could use the police card. Rather than threatening to contact the police yourself, you could tell Jarvis that you can only tell the police the truth if you are questioned about what you know. Yes, such a response might be a prelude to getting fired, but that's better than using a lie to send someone who is possibly innocent to prison and committing a crime in the process. In any event, given the seriousness of the request, you might look into leaving and finding another job anyway, even if Jarvis didn't fire you.

But in either case, why walk away without even asking to get paid? Instead, it is best to at least ask for payment, and if Jarvis shows any hesitation, point out that you earned the money and it is rightfully yours regardless of how you part ways. If that doesn't work, tell Jarvis that you will file a complaint with the appropriate regulatory agencies. Such a strategy will often work, since a boss who is engaged in questionable or criminal behavior will not likely want to have regulators looking into what he is doing. In short, your goal here is to get away as gracefully and quickly as possible, and take the money you have earned with you.

Today's Take-Aways

- ☑ Don't let a boss make you "yes" yourself into committing a crime because going along could mean going to jail yourself.
- ☑ If you have to lie to keep saying yes to your boss, it's time to tell the truth with a no.
- ☑ If your yeses are helping to cloud up what's really going on, it's time to clear up the situation with a loud and clear no.

17 The Wolf in Sheep's Clothing

Sometimes a boss is so bad in so many ways and everyone knows it, yet they feel helpless to do anything due to a hierarchical structure and contract agreements. Such a boss is not just incompetent, insensitive, manipulative, insulting, unfair, and vindictive. He can also be found fraternizing with employees and expecting too much of everyone while taking time off for himself, and much more. While this boss may likely be out of a job eventually, due to reports of his misdeeds to higher-ups and the high turnover of disillusioned underlings, he can continue to wreak havoc for the present because employees feel cowed and don't know what to do. An analogy would be the rolling stone that at first gathers no moss, but gradually accumulates more and more mud until it is finally stuck. Until then, a good strategy is to stay as far as you can from the rolling rock and warn others to do the same, while at the same time helping to heap on the mud.

That's what Shauna experienced when she began her first year of teaching in a K–12 school on a small Indian reservation on the prairies. Though the salary was lower than in the nearby public school and she couldn't earn tenure, she felt inspired by making a public service contribution, and by the charm of the principal, Dr. Ryan, as he explained his philosophy of helping to educate the underprivileged. She felt a few years of teaching in this challenging environment would also help her find a good teaching job in the local public school system.

But soon, Shauna, like many other teachers in the school, began to feel that Dr. Ryan's words were all a sham. In fact, he proved to be incompetent in numerous ways, including in "student relations, public relations, administrative duties, and especially staff relations," according to Shauna. As she described it, Dr. Ryan's incompetence was making her first year of teaching "probably the worst year" in her career.

For one thing, Dr. Ryan regularly demeaned and humiliated the students. He told the fourth grade students they would probably end up in jail or as drunken bums in the gutter and told other elementary school students that they would "amount to nothing better than 'rez dogs.'" When he spoke at assemblies, he used language far above the comprehension level of the younger students, and he often punished those who became restless because they couldn't understand. In certain cases, he was too quick to expel students for discipline problems, even though other staff members felt they could easily deal with the problem.

While Dr. Ryan had a great charm when he talked to the public and was able to impress those with the most influence in the community with his smooth style, he didn't follow through in getting funds or community support for school programs. He also showed a lack of community interest by his failure to attend the cultural events held at the school, such as round dances and feasts.

Worse, some of his actions bordered on criminal, such as using school property and funds for personal use. For example, he used the school van instead of his car. He regularly took it home and drove it to work each day. The drive was a 60-minute round trip that included about five miles on washed-out gravel roads, leaving the van in a battered condition by the end of the school year.

He proved to be a poor administrator, too. He routinely delegated numerous administrative tasks to first-year teachers who didn't realize they should not have been doing those tasks. He took many days off during the entire year, including taking a trip to Cuba that delayed the opening of the school after a school break. On the students' last day of school in June, he spent the day on the golf course.

Shauna also found that Dr. Ryan didn't back up the staff when they had discipline problems in their classrooms. He would blame and humiliate teachers when they had problems, and he didn't discipline the students sent to his office if their parents were influential in the community. When other less well-connected students were sent to the office for discipline, however, he put them to work helping the custodians. This contributed to discipline problems since many students preferred doing this work to being in class.

Dr. Ryan also regularly bullied and harassed the teachers. He was especially abusive to one young teacher he asked out, though he was living with another woman. After she refused him, he frequently yelled at her and reduced her to tears. Still another problem was that he often changed teaching assignments in the first three months of school, when favored teachers requested new assignments, thus leaving many teachers feeling confused and overworked since they had to develop new lessons after a switch.

Additionally, Dr. Ryan pried into teachers' private lives and sought to find out extremely personal information. He would ask them questions about their families, children, and romantic lives. He spoke about other staff members negatively behind their backs. He also had a seven-month affair with one of the first-year teachers and then promoted her to vice principal.

Finally, Dr. Ryan used the teacher evaluations like a club to ensure conformity with his orders and to discourage teachers from resisting or complaining. If staff members did not go along with his requests, he told them it would affect their evaluation. And when Shauna sought to discuss some of her concerns, she faced repeated retaliation from Dr. Ryan for the remainder of the school year, such as when he slandered her to other teachers and to other districts where she was applying for a job for the next year, despite that she had previously received a glowing evaluation.

In short, Dr. Ryan was a nightmare boss. Needless to say, Shauna, like most of the other teachers, was eager to leave. Half of the teachers left that year, and almost everyone else resigned the following year. Fortunately, Shauna found a full-time job in the public school district for the following year due to some personal connections, and later found another job in another county. Though she found her first-year experience horrendous, she also felt she had "learned a lot" and "gained the strength to face anything at work." When she later discovered that Dr. Ryan lost his job at the reservation school and at two other school districts subsequently, and was currently searching for a job, she felt there was some justice after all.

What Should Shauna Have Done?

While Shauna ultimately left after just one year, was there anything she might have done while at the job to improve her situation? In Shauna's place, what would you do and why? What do you think the outcomes of these different options would be? Here are some possibilities:

➲ Start documenting everything and plan to sue for abuse and slander.

➲ Talk to the other teachers who feel similarly abused and send a complaint letter signed by everyone to the school superintendent.

➲ Tell Dr. Ryan you will not accept the way he is treating you and threaten to complain to the superintendent and others, or even sue, if he doesn't treat you better. Start talking to your lawyer or teachers' association.

➲ Set up a meeting with your principal to tell him diplomatically why his disparaging treatment of the children is contributing to discipline problems and upsetting the parents.

➲ Just relax and tune out Dr. Ryan when he says or does things that disturb you. Try to stay on his good side so you get good recommendations to help you get another better job next year.

Unfortunately, this is the kind of situation where you may have little leverage to change your boss's bad behavior, because you are in a large, hierarchical, bureaucratic organization where it can take a very long time to go through complaint procedures. Typically, these will involve assorted hearings and appeals, and your boss will have more power without the backing of other teachers or a teacher's union.

Thus, it may be best to take a more quiet, strategic, long-term approach, looking to leverage yourself into a better job in another school or school district after your contract ends. Since your boss is engaging in a widespread pattern of abusive behavior, trying to have a one-on-one chat could easily backfire and make you a target of even more abuse in the future. This, in fact, is what happened to Shauna when she discussed her concerns with the principal. Shauna followed the district's Code of Conduct for raising such issues, but Dr. Ryan still retaliated. Gone were the glowing evaluations as he began slandering her to other school districts during reference checks.

In this situation, a better approach might be to observe things quietly in a calm, detached way, creating a sense of distance from the principal's reign of terror. Then, as you act like nothing is wrong, you gather and document what he has done to abuse you and others. Meanwhile, as best you can, let other trusted teachers know what you are doing and invite them to do the same, since there is safety in numbers.

You might also give comfort to the organization's clients who have been abused or insulted—in this case the junior high students—so they don't take the put-downs to heart. And you might comfort other teachers so they feel better, too, perhaps even creating a small support group among coworkers who feel as you do.

Another approach would be to gather with your coworkers and plan your strategy as a group. For example, if you all document these incidents, you will be in a better position to collectively take action against the boss, such as by setting up a group meeting to ask for changes. Or if such a meeting seems too risky due to retaliation that could affect your employment, wait until the recommendations for the year are in and then complain as a group. This way, at least you help to get the bad boss out of the system so he can't abuse others in the future.

Today's Take-Aways

- ☑ If your boss is a wolf in sheep's clothing, find ways to pull off the wool without being seen.
- ☑ If you can't get improvements now, trying getting even later.
- ☑ If your boss is bad news for everyone, look for ways to end your subscriptions together.
- ☑ Just as you might try to make the best of a bad situation, try to make the best of a bad boss by finding ways to detach. Don't take it personally.

18

Controlling the Control Freak

At the opposite extreme from the disorganized, inefficient, or inept boss is the power-hungry control freak. When this boss is the company owner in a small company, the problem is doubly worse as there's no one upstairs to appeal to. It's just you and the control freak. With more and more companies today being small businesses and start-ups—over 50% of the economy —the potential for this problem is much greater. In the corporate, team-player environment, you are likely to find more controls on out-of-control behavior, as well as coworkers with whom to commiserate, but the small business run by a control freak can be a treacherous, lonely place. However, when you need the job and otherwise like the work, it can be worth trying to take some of the control yourself.

That's what happened for Tammy. She was hired as a marketing assistant by an artist, Patrick. Patrick wanted to arrange for his work to be shown in galleries and secure contracts for posters, greeting cards, and corporate design work. Tammy's job was to locate contacts, call or write them, and pitch his work. She had previously worked at a series of small galleries as a gallery assistant, where her main responsibilities were keeping up the database, filing, and greeting customers; this job was definitely a step up. She also she loved the high level of responsibility and autonomy when Patrick was in his studio working. But whenever he showed up, she felt overwhelmed and belittled. He would bark out a series of precise orders, criticize her, and even tell her what to do in her personal life.

For example, once after she had written up and printed out a series of letters, he told her they were all wrong. The margins she had used were too small; he wanted them set to 1.4″ rather than the 1.25″ standard format. He also berated her for answering the phone with a simple "Hello, Patrick's Art Works," as she had been doing for a couple of weeks. "That's too abrupt," he screamed at her, "You need to take more time to say it, and add in 'award-winning.'" Another time, as she walked in the office, he began criticizing her appearance, telling her: "Your lipstick is too dark. You should wear a lighter tone," and "You'd look better if you let your hair grow longer and if you wore more colorful clothes."

At times, Tammy tried to explain or protest, but Patrick generally got defensive and yelled back even louder, screaming such things as, "Why can't you listen?" or "I'm the boss here!" Tammy would back down and listen to his tirades in silence. Then, a few minutes after Patrick's explosion of orders or anger, it was as though a storm had passed and the sun came out and shone brightly. Though Patrick never apologized, suddenly he was all cheeriness and smiles again. He would praise Tammy for something she did well, give her an assignment for another project, and go off to his office to work. After Tammy calmed down from the latest tirade, she was able to go back to work. However, her nerves were still frayed, and she was left wondering when the next explosion might occur.

But Tammy didn't want to quit. She felt the position would open up doors into the art world that would be hard to match in another job. Art jobs were hard to find and she did truly admire Patrick's work, if not his behavior. Yet the frequent upsets at work often left her feeling on edge and anxious. She worried that the tense feeling in her stomach could even turn into an ulcer.

What Should Tammy Do?

In Tammy's place, what would you do and why? What do you think the outcomes of these different options would be? Here are some possibilities:

➲ Steel yourself for the next confrontation with Patrick, and the next time he seems out of line, yell back more loudly to show him you won't take his tirades anymore.

- ⇒ Set up a meeting with Patrick when he is calm and rational. Quietly and diplomatically explain how much you like the job but that you feel hurt when he yells at you, and ask what might be done to remedy the situation.

- ⇒ Document the times when Patrick is out of control and send him a memo describing each incident and why you feel this is inappropriate.

- ⇒ Whenever Patrick gives you an assignment, ask him to tell you very clearly exactly how he wants you to do it.

- ⇒ Tell Patrick you feel it is fine for him to correct you at work, but that it isn't appropriate for him to make comments about your appearance or dress.

- ⇒ Inform Patrick that his behavior is abusive and a form of workplace harassment and he should stop. If he threatens to fire you, tell him that retaliatory termination is illegal.

- ⇒ Learn to live with Patrick's tirades, He is just a high-strung creative artist, and bring some bicarbonates to work to take for your jangled nerves and stomach.

The trick here is to control Patrick's out-of-control behavior without escalating the situation any further. Your goal is to create a smoother working environment without alienating the boss. Sure, Tammy could simply learn to take it like a wet sponge, getting repeatedly squashed by Patrick. But it is better not to take Patrick's tirades personally. Instead, consider that they may be due to a number of factors that have nothing to do with you, such as Patrick's insecurities about making the best impression on others, a long tradition of being a compulsive perfectionist, or his emotional style of expressing himself. So that's why he's so concerned about such things as exactly how his letters look on page, what Tammy says on the phone, and what she wears and blasts off when something upsets his vision of exactly how things should be.

Certainly, some of his demands are excessive and inappropriate, but the best way to create a better relationship is not to attack him for making such demands. Directly challenging him will make him more defensive and is likely to trigger more attacks. Also, since Patrick is an artist and seems to have a more visual and verbal style of relating, written memos are probably not a good way to go. They will seem too impersonal when what you really need is a real heart-to-heart. You want to get your concerns on the table, but in a nonthreatening way.

Try setting up a meeting early in the day, before Patrick has a chance to get upset or angry about anything. When you sit down with Patrick explain that you want to share some of your concerns with a view to helping you do a better job. In other words, emphasize how you want to help him, and point out how he can help you do that, such as by telling you in advance specifically what he wants when he assigns a project (e.g., what size margins he wants on a letter). Also, explain that it would be helpful to have some general guidelines for what to say in greeting and meeting prospective clients, such as what to say when you answer the phone. And ask him to give you some guidelines for what he feels is appropriate office dress, though point out that as long as you dress professionally, you feel you should be allowed to express your own style. Diplomatically and calmly explain how you have felt hurt by his comments criticizing your style. This way, you focus on your feelings rather than accusing Patrick directly of insulting behavior.

Sure, Patrick has been a boor, but you don't want to tell him that directly. As they say, you can attract more flies with honey than vinegar. Therefore, use honeyed words to keep things calm. You want to control Patrick's behavior, not swat him down. Perhaps another way to think of Patrick is as a boiling pot that occasionally boils over. You want to be able to turn down the heat to stop the pot from boiling.

Today's Take-Aways

☑ When someone is upset and out-of-control, the best way to get control is to stay calm and in control of yourself first. Use charm rather than challenge to stay in control.

☑ When you work with a boss that frequently gets hot and bothered, find a way to turn down the heat.

☑ When someone has a particular style of relating, use that style to communicate your messages about the changes you want; such messages are more likely to get through. For example, don't send a memo if someone has a more visual and verbal style of relating.

To get someone out of your face, try a little quality face time instead of a face-off. That way you can put your concerns on the table and are more likely to be heard. Throwing them back in someone's face could lead to your having egg on yours.

19

Bad Boss in a Big Bureaucracy

What happens when you've got a bad boss and most of your coworkers agree, but a layered bureaucracy and procedural protections make it very hard to dislodge that boss for anything other than grossly out-of-line behavior? If the boss merely creates a corrosive, demoralizing environment that may not be enough to get him ousted, leaving you and the other employees feeling stuck and frustrated, and griping to each other. This situation is more common of governmental and educational bureaucracies, where all kinds of rules and procedures are in place for handling complaints. But what do you do if it happens to you? Endure and suffer? Or can you take steps to make the problem go away more quickly?

Morris, a college teacher in his late thirties, faced such a situation when he was working at a state university. Adam, the dean of the college, had come to the school with glowing recommendations from his previous schools. He had been the director of a research facility, was nationally known for his studies in his field, and had taught for over a decade at three different universities with stellar reputations.

But Morris and other faculty members soon began to feel Adam created a hostile work environment. They complained that he put down faculty and staff members with insults, not only at private one-on-one meetings but also at gatherings of the whole department. At faculty meetings, he would say outrageous things to some of the teachers such as, "You're a real bitch," and "How did you ever get hired at a university? You're so dumb." Many faculty members also complained that Adam "played favorites with funding and resources," so he gave more money and equipment to the teachers who sweetly "sucked up" to him by praising his decisions and never challenging his choices.

For the first two years, Morris and the other teachers griped privately among themselves. Then, the faculty association filed a complaint with the Equal Employment Opportunity Commission, which agreed to hire an outside consultant to review the situation. Although the commission recommended that Adam be put on leave for six to twelve months, nothing happened. It was as if the commission had not made any recommendation at all. The same harassing environment continued, with many of the faculty who initiated the complaint even more edgy, thinking they would be treated even worse.

Finally, in the face of this bureaucratic inaction, about two dozen tenured professors including Morris came together to write and send a letter to the university president and provost saying they had "no confidence" in the dean. Soon after that Adam resigned, supposedly to spend time on writing a book while remaining a tenured faculty member. As a result, he was still around, though he was no longer dean. This arrangement left Morris and other faculty members who filed the letter uncomfortable about possible repercussions for their actions. One professor who signed the letter told the media she hoped Adam's departure as dean would help the college heal, come together, and move forward. But Morris and the other faculty members were concerned about the situation, since Adam still had his faculty position and reputation from previous teaching assignments.

What Should Morris Have Done and What Should He Do Now?

Is there anything Morris might have done differently? In Morris's place, what would you do and why? What do you think the outcomes of these different options would be? Here are some possibilities:

➲ Avoid contact with Adam as much as possible so his behavior doesn't bother you so much.

➲ Talk to some other faculty members early on to begin the process of getting rid of Adam before he is in such a strong power position at the school.

➲ Create a committee of faculty members to talk to Adam as a group to explain what is bothering everyone and ask Adam to change.

➲ Contact the local media anonymously to tell them that most of the teachers are very unhappy with the school's abusive environment and that there may be a good story in this situation. The media pressure may persuade Adam to change or leave sooner.

➲ Grin and bear it, since it's best to stay out of faculty politics to get ahead in your career.

➲ Check from time to time to make sure Adam isn't still trying to influence school policy as a professor. Call him on this at faculty meetings and advise other faculty members to do the same.

The unwieldy bureaucracy and procedures for making any changes at the university contribute to the difficult situation As a result, you are in a system that is quite resistant to change, and you have a relatively low power position to make any changes by yourself. Accordingly, a good initial strategy is to stay out of Adam's crosshairs as much as possible by continuing to do a good job teaching and doing research. Also, it may be best to keep quiet in public if Adam is not amenable to being challenged at meetings. You don't want to stand up if you're only going to be easily shut down, if other teachers feel too cowed to speak up themselves or to help someone else in challenging the dean.

But while remaining publicly quiet, you might arrange to talk privately with other faculty members early on. Do this within the first six months of when the abusive behavior begins rather than waiting two years to file a complaint. A group meeting with Adam to talk over problems might be a good first step. If he doesn't respond by making any changes, then it might be time to file a formal complaint during this initial six-month period. That's better than waiting for two years, which gives Adam time to become even more rigid and out of touch in enforcing his policies.

It is also a good idea for all of the teachers who experience abusive treatment to keep a diary or journal tracking these occurrences. This way there is a clear, documented record that can be used in the many hearings required in a government or education bureaucracy to fire anyone (or encourage someone to step down). Sending a letter is good, too, in the event a formal body like the EEOC doesn't pursue the initial complaint about the abuse. But just as you should file the complaint in this initial six-month period, so should you send the "no confidence" letter to the president or other top official of your school during this time frame.

In short, if you've got a bad boss in a slow-moving bureaucratic setting and want to stay because you like the job, act more quickly to deal with the problem. Since it normally takes months of meetings and hearings for anything to happen, especially something as serious as firing the boss, start early because the process will move like molasses. And consider ways to speed up the process by bringing in the voice of the media or the public, as this could put pressure on the bureaucracy to act now to discipline or terminate the boss.

Today's Take-Aways

☑ If it's going to be a long process to get rid of a bad boss, get an early start so you don't have to wait.

☑ When the inner workings of an organization usually move slowly, try to get some outer influences to help speed up the process.

☑ If you've got a rolling stone of a boss who is rolling over everyone and gathering no moss, come together to stop the rolling and then the moss will stick.

☑ Think of a big bureaucracy as a slow-moving train; if enough people get on the tracks, you can force the train to change tracks.

Breaking Through the Bureaucracy

Sometimes a boss can be too rigid, feeling it necessary to enforce the company rules even when it might be more productive to stretch or change the rules. As the employee, you need to decide if you will follow the rules, because that's the easiest way to go, or work to change the rules so you can be more productive.

Often you can accomplish change if you can show there is a better way to do something that can pay off with superior results. Yet, whenever you are dealing with change, you are also dealing with vested interests in the current ways of doing things. And when employees come up with ideas for change, those in senior positions can feel threatened despite the potential for improved productivity. After all, they are supposed to be the ones with the additional knowledge and power, so they may shut out employee input about a better way to do things.

That's what happened for Drew when he got a job as a research project director in a large public relations firm. Drew was working for Jackson, the director of the research department. Drew's job was to take responsibility for a whole project from start to finish. Occasionally, he met with fellow project directors to share information about what they were each doing and traded resources and contact information, such as the names of outside research facilitators and pollsters to whom they subcontracted some of the work.

Drew soon found that, with the exception of these meetings with the project directors, he got a lot more done working at home. Much of his job consisted of writing up reports, and it was hard to concentrate in the office. His desk at work was located with a dozen other desks in a large open area shared by both Jackson and the secretarial pool. Not only was there a continuous, low-level buzz in the office from conversations, ringing phones, and files opening and closing, but there were other distractions, such as people stopping by his desk with questions. In contrast, Drew could write without interruption at home, and if he needed to call local suppliers or vendors, or receive calls from them, he could easily do so.

At first, Jackson seemed to go along with Drew's proposal to work at home and just come in for meetings. Not only would Drew be able to turn in more high-quality reports, but Jackson seemed pleased with his work.

But after about three weeks, Jackson called Drew into the office and told him that the work at home would have to stop. Why, Drew wanted to know? Because, Jackson explained, "other people in the office are wondering why you can do this, and they may want to work at home, too. They feel it's unfair for you to come and go whenever you want, when they can't. So from now on, you have to come in at 9 a.m. like everyone else and work till 5 p.m., no exceptions."

Though Drew nodded his head in agreement, he was very resentful, feeling that Jackson should have stood up for him to support his special out-of-the-office work arrangement since it was working so well. Though Drew came into the office the next few days and tried to work there, he felt demoralized and dispirited. He felt like he wanted to be anywhere else, since his dream job had turned into a nightmare. He blamed Jackson's follow-the-rules rigidity for what happened. So Drew was faced with a dilemma: Should he try to work on accepting what happened and go along with the decision? Or should he fight it?

What Should Drew Do?

In Drew's place, what would you do and why? What do you think the outcomes of these different options would be? Here are some possibilities:

- ⮞ Talk to the other research project directors to explain what you are doing and show that you were really working harder at home, not slacking off.

- ⮞ Write up a detailed memo to Jackson to argue for your ability to work at home so Jackson has something to show to the higher-ups to support your arguments for keeping the work-at-home arrangement.

- ⮞ Tell Jackson about your feelings of frustration at the new enforcement policy and ask him what you might do to help convince the higher-ups and others in your department that you should be allowed to work at home.

- ⮞ Argue to Jackson that if it is more efficient for you to work at home, maybe it might be more efficient for others and suggest that they should be given this option.

- ⮞ Send a memo to the higher-ups in the company, telling them why you have found it more efficient to work it home and how it might help the company if others were given this option.

The best approach here depends very much on the personalities and politics of the particular office. Jackson seems to be a comfortable, easy-to-get-along-with type of guy. He initially went along with Drew's proposal to work in a different way, and it proved to be quite effective. But later, he lacked the backbone to go to bat for the new approach by either explaining how well it was working to top management or to Drew's coworkers. If he had done so, the fate of Drew's work-at-home days might have been different.

Unfortunately, the situation led Drew—once a model employee who loved his job—to turn into a difficult one who hated it. This is something that often occurs when bad boss behavior meets worker resistance, and it can lead to an employee's individual and usually misguided efforts to bring justice to a situation he considers unfair. For example, in Drew's case, he soon started finding ways to take extra time for himself on the job, such as taking extra-long coffee breaks and using some supplies from the art department for his own projects. Meanwhile, the quality of his work began to suffer. His mind was elsewhere, and not just because of the distractions in the office. Drew had lost his enthusiasm for the job, and his declining performance soon showed, ultimately leading to a warning from

Jackson to improve or get out. Drew responded by giving notice one week later.

Such a deteriorating situation might have never occurred had Jackson been more sensitive and flexible in the situation, especially since Drew really had been turning in excellent work. For example, if Jackson could show top managers how Drew's more flexible work approach led to better quality work and helped the bottom line, they might have realized the benefits of allowing the arrangement to continue. Moreover, they might have even considered that it was worth giving some other employees this same option if they felt their job lent itself to working at home. Furthermore, if Jackson had defended Drew's arrangement at a meeting with the other research project directors, this might have reassured them that Drew was really working much harder and doing a better job as a result. Once Drew's coworkers were more comfortable, that might have put an end to the resistance.

However, Jackson did none of these things on his own. If you are faced with a situation like Drew's, a good approach might be to suggest that Jackson use the above strategies to appeal to both the company's top executives and to the other project directors. This way, he could show how you are doing a better job for the company by working at home and reassure the other employees that you aren't slacking off. Perhaps if they also had the option of working at home, they could do an equally good job.

It probably would not work to try to go above Jackson to appeal directly to the company officers, since they were the ones who put up the roadblock that Jackson implemented. Your focus should be on convincing Jackson to intervene to benefit the company. Moreover, you might try meeting with Jackson to share your frustrations and anger about the new arrangements rather than letting your resentments boil over into hurtful sabotage. Keep in mind that you could help to sabotage your own career should your sabotage be discovered.

If none of these tactics were successful, you might find a way to channel your frustration and anger into something more productive than undercutting your good performance and swiping materials from the company's art department. You might continue to do a good job, though not as good as if working from home. Over time, you might try to make the case by comparing what you accomplished when working at home with what you are accomplishing now that you have to work in the office. With additional evidence of your increased productivity working at home, you could appeal Jackson's initial decision by making a stronger case to support your desired change.

Today's Take-Aways

☑ Instead of letting a boss who is unnecessarily rigid in support of the company bureaucracy get you down, look for ways to beat back that bureaucracy by showing why your way is better for the bottom line.

☑ If your boss doesn't initially come to bat for you, try handing him the bat and showing him how to use it.

☑ If your boss isn't strong enough to stand up for your really good ideas, show strength yourself to make your boss stronger. Think of yourself as the good soldier who will help your boss win the war, and show him how you can help him win it.

☑ Don't try to get even through sabotage; instead, try to get what you really want through strength.

Since out of sight can be out of mind, do something to make the work you are doing at home known to top management. Once you're no longer out of sight, they will see how good it is.

21

It Goes with the Territory

In some cases, bosses may be bad because of the requirements and culture of the industry, and you can't do much to change the situation if you want to continue working in that industry. Though things may be improving due to protective legislation, this may not be helpful on a day-to-day basis. A great many people in a particular field may complain about bad bosses, but they have learned to put up with it because that's just the way things are. The boss has a huge amount of power while they have very little. And the field is so competitive that if they challenge their bad treatment, they know there are thousands of other people just like them waiting to get their job.

That was the difficulty facing Meredith when she got a job in the film industry working as a first assistant director. While the director worked primarily with the actors, the second assistant director handled routine behind-the-scenes paperwork and props, so Meredith's job was the real nuts and bolts of getting everything ready on the set. She had to coordinate all the logistics to help the director get the shot he wanted, which meant telling everyone on camera where to go, making sure the prop people had the props in place, telling the camera people where to set up the cameras, and the like. Meanwhile, the director would bark out orders to her on her small radio, which was always turned on so she could immediately respond to him. Besides the high level of stress from moment to moment, the job was an incredibly grueling one. Meredith's typical schedule involved working from 4 a.m. until 2 a.m. the next morning, driving back to the hotel, getting about an hour of sleep, and returning to the set the next day to do it all over again.

Her big complaint was that the director, Brad, was like a dictator or tyrant. He ordered her and others around, regardless of how tired people were, and in spite of the potential dangers of working with large machinery or in difficult terrain. Yet, as difficult as Brad was, his behavior wasn't unique in the industry; all directors were driven to get those great shots. So like many others in the film industry, Meredith sucked in her feelings of anger and resentment and shared her stories of tyranny on the set with others—a kind of misery-loves-company approach to releasing her feelings.

Eventually, all that anger boiled over. Meredith had gotten everything ready on the set, everyone on the crew knew what to do, and there would be a few minutes downtime before the actors were on set and the cameras ready to shoot. Feeling everything was done, Meredith headed off for a much-needed bathroom break in one of the small motor homes near the set. She had just sat down on the toilet seat, when Brad's voice came booming over the radio: "Where the f**k are you?" Meredith explained she was in the bathroom, but Brad didn't seem to want to hear it. "People don't know what to do!" he screamed. "You've got to get back here immediately." Of course, Meredith knew full well that the people *did* know what to do, and that no immediate crisis existed. Brad was simply being unreasonable, and she let him rant on for another 30 seconds or so until she was ready to leave the bathroom.

But it was a defining moment for her. In that moment, she made a decision to quit. "This is a lousy industry," she told herself. "I'm out of here." Meredith reflected on how the film industry was such an one, particularly toward women, and how conditions had been bad for so long that those in the industry seemed to generally accept them. But she didn't want to put up with it anymore. She no longer wanted to work for Brad or any other of the industry's bad bosses. So a few days later, she turned in her resignation. She had had enough.

What Should Meredith Have Done?

Is there anything Meredith might have done differently? In Meredith's place, what would you do and why? What do you think the outcomes of these different options would be? Here are some possibilities:

- ⮩ Turn off the radio when you are in the restroom so Brad would not be able to berate you.

- ⮩ Tell Brad in advance when you have to leave for a much-needed bathroom break. Reassure him that everything is ready, that everybody knows what they are doing, and that you'll be back in about 90 seconds.

- ⮩ Stand up to Brad immediately when he yells or screams at you rather than just taking it. This way he will understand it's unacceptable to treat you this way.

- ⮩ Continue to accept that this is the way things are in the industry and go back to work like nothing had happened.

- ⮩ Go along with Brad's demands, quickly apologize and make nice when he yells, and commiserate with others about how bad things are so you feel better.

- ⮩ Contact the Director's Guild to complain about Brad's irrational behavior and hope they can do something.

There may be little Meredith could have done in the short term other than going along to get along, and when the situation finally got to be too much to cope with, quit. Unfortunately, outwardly glamorous industries such as the film or music business are notoriously very hard on novices who are trying to get ahead. Because the competition for these entry-level positions is tremendous—Meredith reported that there had been five thousand applicants for her position—those who get these coveted jobs learn early on they'll have to do pretty much whatever any employer asks if they don't want to be replaced. Meanwhile, their bosses are under intense pressure themselves to provide the creative product that drives the industry, so being tough, demanding, or even a slave driver is considered the norm. All of this pressure combined with these mercurial creative personalities can lead to irrational outbursts that would likely not be tolerated in other industries. But as long as the boss turns out the product, that person can usually continue to find assignments in the industry and there will always be a long line of underlings waiting to be given the chance to work on them.

If you are in Meredith's shoes, you may have to simply accept this bad behavior as something that comes with the territory if you want to continue working in this industry. Perhaps down the road, if motivated, you can be more proactive. For example, after gaining more power and connections in the industry, you might stand up to an unreasonable director and ask to be treated with more respect. You could explain that you will be glad to do whatever he wants, but ask that he refrain from yelling and screaming at you, since you can do a better job if he just calmly tells you what to do.

In this case, it might have been good to prepare Brad in advance for your need to take a quick break and explain that everything is ready for him. But otherwise, simply enduring and detaching yourself from Brad's ranting might be the way to go; it would be less stressful to let his tirade wash over you like "water off a duck's back." It might not work well to try turning off the radio, because if you did so, there would be consequences. As soon as you reappeared with your radio back on, Brad would be on your case, and there might be further penalties. You could even lose your job only to be quickly replaced by one of the thousands of wannabes in the industry. And it might assuage the pain of quietly taking it by commiserating with others who feel similarly about the abuse they have suffered.

This kind of response might not be what to do when you have a similarly manic and abusive boss in another industry, where there is a greater spirit of fairness, empowered employees, and employer accountability. But here, where the industry is generally filled with freelancers, sparse regulation, and a large cadre of wannabes, there is little you can do to change the very difficult conditions. If you can't change your boss in a culture that inspires and supports bad bosses, the choice is basically between these options: (1) Accept what you can't change for now and do the best you can to endure, lowering the stress by finding ways to relax and perhaps sharing with others, (2) Gracefully find a way to get out, (3) Hope for a better boss despite the industry odds against it, or (4) Find another field in which to work.

Today's Take-Aways

☑ Keep in mind some popular sayings: "If you can't beat them join them." "When in Rome, do as the Romans do." "Learn to go with the flow." Make these your mantras.

☑ If you want to get along, go along, but if you can't go along, get out.

☑ An abusive work culture is like a raging river: You can't change the way the current flows, but you can learn to ride it and keep from going under.

☑ When nature sends you a hurricane, duck for cover, get out of the way, and ride out the storm.

☑ If something's too big for you, you may not be able to fight on your own. In the long run, however, you may be able to create change with some outside and expert help.

Who's the Boss?

Working for two bosses can sometimes be very confusing, particularly when the bosses have different styles, don't like each other, and give conflicting orders. You may be uncertain how to prioritize your work, how to meet differing expectations, and how to avoid the crossfire when the bosses fight. Individually, each boss might be fine to work for, once you adapt to his particular way of doing things. But put them together and you have two bad bosses.

That's what happened to Estelle when she got a job as an administrative assistant for two attorneys in a large firm devoted to criminal defense work and plaintiff litigation. Her job was to fill out the assorted documents needed for court (such as motions and subpoenas), file the necessary papers on time, make copies and file documents, and keep track of each attorney's cases in a database. Sometimes she even got to sit in on the cases and observe. Estelle liked the job and had her sights set on becoming a paralegal and eventually a lawyer, but she soon found it difficult to sort out which work she was supposed to do when and for whom. This presented a big problem, since it was critical for her to meet the case deadlines. Missed deadlines could translate into losing a case.

The first sign of trouble came the week she started, working at a small desk in the office shared by the two attorneys, Barry and Andrea. Estelle noticed right away that the two sides of the office were very different. While Barry's desk was piled high with papers and books and files were scattered across the desk, Andrea's side was neat as a pin. The desk was cleared off except for a plastic file box with a few files that Andrea was currently working on.

That first morning, Andrea spent a few hours telling Estelle about how the law firm handled the litigation process. She also told her that Barry was out of town on vacation for the week, but would be back in a few days. Then, she gave Estelle her first assignment, which was to write up and send out subpoenas for two upcoming cases. Estelle immediately started in on Andrea's cases, feeling good about her new job and new boss, while Andrea went off to court for the afternoon.

That afternoon, as she was typing up a dozen subpoenas, she got a call from Barry who sounded frantic. He briefly told her that he was sorry to be out of town and wasn't there to meet her on her first day. But now he had a crisis and needed her help to complete some documents for a motion he had started. "Otherwise, the case will be dropped," he explained, "so please, please, can you do this now?"

"Sure," Estelle agreed, wanting to be accommodating. She began working on Barry's motion right away.

However, before she could finish it, Andrea returned from court and wanted to know how Estelle was coming with the documents she had left with her. When Estelle told her about Barry's phone call and emergency, Andrea exploded. "But I'm here and I told you what to do. You shouldn't have listened to Barry," she told Estelle.

So Estelle turned back to doing Andrea's work, while Andrea left for a meeting. Then, just as Estelle was about to leave for the evening, she got another call from Barry asking if the project was done. When she said it wasn't because Andrea told her to put her own project first, Barry told her angrily: "But I told you how critical this was. These papers have to be filed tomorrow morning, or the case is lost." After pleading with her to finish the motion, he explained about how he and Andrea sometimes had problems working together, and it was too bad she had to get caught up in this struggle on her first day on the job.

In the end, Estelle cancelled her plans for the evening to finish Barry's motion after Andrea had left for the day. Over the next weeks, Estelle found herself continually having to juggle her heavy workload, trying to meet the competing demands of her two bosses.

But she never knew whose work was more important or what should she do first. To keep the peace, Estelle frequently worked during her lunch hour or stayed late to finish projects when neither attorney was there.

Estelle felt helpless, though, to know what to do when both Barry and Andrea were in the office arguing. Not only did Barry and Andrea argue about whose work should get Estelle's immediate attention, but they also sometimes hurled insults at each other, with Estelle feeling trapped in the middle. "You are such a slob! I hate having to share an office with you! I can't believe how you can ever find anything on your desk!" Andrea screamed on one such occasion. "And you, you're such an obsessive-compulsive neat freak!" Barry yelled back. "Please, give me a break!"

Later, after the argument had died down, Andrea and Barry went to Estelle privately to complain about the other. The two bosses each pointed out how the other one was such a difficult person to work with. Estelle felt caught in the middle, though she liked each boss individually for different reasons. Barry was great because he had such an easygoing, friendly, cheerful nature. She liked Andrea because she was so well-organized and took time to teach her about the legal process like a personal mentor. But together they were like fire and ice, oil and water, continually coming into conflict with each other. She didn't know what to do about it and felt a growing stress from the job.

In Estelle's case, the problem finally resolved itself after three months of growing tension when Andrea got a promotion and was moved to another office. Estelle was reassigned to work under another attorney in another department in the law firm. Still, there are some steps Estelle might have taken to address the problem directly before it resolved itself.

What Should Estelle Have Done?

In Estelle's place, what would you do and why? What do you think the outcomes of these different options would be? Here are some possibilities:

➲ Tell both Andrea and Barry that you don't want to hear them complaining about each other.

⊃   Ask Andrea and Barry to have a meeting to discuss their prob-
    lems with each other to work out some solution. Offer to medi-
    ate the discussion.

⊃   Speak to one of the partners in the law firm who assigns offices
    and tell that person what is going on; maybe he will assign An-
    drea and Barry to different offices.

⊃   Tune out Andrea and Barry when they fight or when they try to
    tell you negative information about each other. Figure it's their
    problem, not yours; this way you will feel less stress.

⊃   Do your assignments in the order you receive them, and tell An-
    drea and Barry this is what you'll be doing. If either wants you
    to give their project first priority, he or she will have to check
    with the other to get their okay before you change the order of
    what you are doing.

⊃   Ask Andrea and Barry to clarify when their assignments are due
    and create a chart to help you prioritize. You can use this chart
    as a guide when you have conflicting instructions from Andrea
    and Barry.

A number of strategies might have helped to ease the tension in this
situation. Separating Andrea and Barry would have been an ideal
option, and that's what eventually happened when Andrea was promoted. But as a new lower-level employee such as Estelle, you probably shouldn't try directly appealing to higher-level officers in the
firm. Not only might the officers see this action as inappropriate, but
Andrea and Barry could consider this a betrayal and start directing
their animosity toward you as well as each other.

A conflict resolution session between Andrea and Barry might
also have helped to release steam and help them work out a better
way of relating to each other and handling contradictory assignments. However, you probably shouldn't try to mediate the conflict
between them since you are a lower-level employee working for both
of them. Any such offer to do so might be viewed by either Andrea
or Barry as presumptuous, as well as a threat to their own authority
over you.

However, what might help is to stop giving Andrea and Barry
any support for their attacks on each other. You could tell Andrea
and Barry individually that you feel uncomfortable when they share

their complaints about each other with you. At the same time, you might try tuning out their arguments by focusing on your work or using that time to do something outside of the shared office, such as copying documents on the hall copier or filing documents at court. Making a schedule of assignments and prioritizing them, then discussing this plan with both Andrea and Barry, would also help. In this case, a good approach would be to explain that you are setting up this master schedule because you want to improve the workflow and meet their deadlines. Then, if you can get their buy-in, you become in charge of coordinating the schedule, rather than reacting to spontaneous and frequently conflicting demands from both Andrea and Barry. This way, you can more clearly show both of them exactly what you are doing and when, thus reducing or avoiding altogether the late-night or weekend hours required to meet unexpected deadlines.

In short, think of more systematic ways to reduce the sources of the tension between the two bosses. Don't contribute to the division by listening to their complaints against each other. Tune out any conflict that occurs by mentally focusing elsewhere, such as on your work. Or try physically removing yourself from the setting. If you must, find reasons to do some of your work outside the office, or take a break for coffee or lunch.

Today's Take-Aways

☑ If you can't clear the air with clear communication, try clearing out for awhile. Things may have cleared up when you get back.

☑ When you are working for two bosses whose styles and personalities don't mix very well, try to stay focused and out of the fray, so you don't mix things up any more.

☑ When you're finding it hard to please two masters, see if you can master your own schedule, and use that to organize and prioritize what your two masters want you to do.

Part IV

Out of Bounds

Dirty Looks

Today, with all the regulations and sexual harassment lawsuits in the workplace, you wouldn't think bosses would still engage in so-called "lewd and lascivious" behavior. Yet some bosses (usually men) still do. And when they are particularly important and powerful, they may get away with this, even when employees (usually women) complain. One reason they do so is that when employees fear losing their jobs, particularly in a tight job market, many stifle their complaints or don't follow through when an initial complaint is not acted upon. So the situation continues, while employees feel violated, angry, or anxious, yet don't know what to do.

That's the problem Audrey faced when she worked for about a year at a research lab. She started out as the secretary to the director who was in charge of 250 researchers. But after a reorganization of the lab, she had a new boss, Ray, who soon became hard to deal with because of the way he looked at her and the other women employees. He also engaged in a number of suggestive and offensive acts. As Audrey described it:

> *He would talk to my breasts, and most of the other women experienced this, too. He sometimes farted in front of me, or when I handed him something, he would scratch his privates. I found his behavior rude and unnerving, as did the other women. In my 30*

years of working for different organizations, I had never seen anything like this, and I was truly shocked.

Initially, Audrey wasn't sure what to do. The first few times Ray stared or did something offensive, she left his office feeling upset, hoping this was an out-of-character exception, just an inadvertent look. She also thought Ray was a good manager otherwise, and that he managed the resources and logistics for many programs well.

But when the behavior continued, Audrey decided she had to do something. She was afraid to confront Ray directly because his behavior made her so nervous, and she feared being fired if she stood up to him. As a result, she complained to Ray's supervisor who managed the whole lab, and a few other women complained as well. That seemed to resolve the problem at first, and for the next two to three months, Ray was on his best behavior. After that, however, Ray reverted to his old ways, perhaps because he felt sufficient time had passed since the initial admonition. The "dirty looks" boss was back to his old tricks.

Once again, the women felt uncomfortable around Ray, but they were unsure whether to complain about him again. They feared losing their jobs, especially since their original complaints hadn't worked. So the women never complained directly to Ray or tried to approach his supervisor again. Instead, they began finding their own ways to stave off his inappropriate looks. For example, when another woman told Audrey that she was "flabbergasted" after leaving Ray's office because he was staring at her crotch, Audrey told her to walk in carrying books in front of her.

The women could have taken their complaint to the next level by filing a formal complaint to the organization's director or legal counsel. If that failed, they might have pursued legal action for sexual harassment or a hostile working environment, and they would have had a good chance at winning since Ray's behavior was clearly beyond the acceptable. Yet no one did anything further, and after seven months of having Ray as her boss, Audrey left the job. She felt she had had enough of his unacceptable behavior.

What Should Audrey Have Done?

Is there anything Audrey might have done differently or something she could do now? In Audrey's place, what would you do and why?

What do you think the outcomes of these different options would be? Here are some possibilities:

➲ Stand up to Ray after the second or third time he does something offensive. Let him know you don't appreciate him looking at you in a suggestive way. Tell him he's in the wrong so you're on firm legal ground if he doesn't stop.

➲ Keep a journal documenting each time Ray looks at you inappropriately or engages in lewd or lascivious behavior, and encourage the other women to do the same. Then you can back up your complaints with documentation.

➲ Complain even more firmly a second time to Ray's supervisor when the intolerable behavior starts again. Emphasize that you and the other women employees are ready to file a formal complaint unless it stops.

➲ Stare directly into Ray's eyes when he stares at you until he becomes uncomfortable and looks away.

➲ Get a group of women together, stare at Ray's crotch together, and laugh. He should get the message from that.

➲ Contact a friend in the media (or one who can sound like someone in the media) who can call Ray and say he is considering doing a story about how Ray has been harassing women and how they are considering suing. That should scare Ray enough that he will stop his dirty looks, comments and behavior.

➲ Warn Ray and his supervisor that you and the other women are about to file a formal complaint if Ray's obnoxious behavior doesn't stop. Follow through in a few days if he doesn't cease and desist.

➲ Dress more conservatively and don't pay attention to Ray's boorish behavior, so his staring and rude remarks don't bother you.

In this case, what Ray is doing is clearly wrong. He is creating a harassing and hostile work environment for the women at the lab. And because there have been no real consequences for his actions, the behavior has continued. After all, the first complaint against him only led to a brief talking-to by his supervisor, which obviously had no effect. Ray felt he could go back to his old behavior, and he was right, since no one else complained again. Rather than fearing for your job—especially if you stick together with the other women—you and the others should stand up to Ray once it is clear from the repeated behavior that Ray isn't acting unintentionally. By the second or third time he says or does anything inappropriate, ask him to stop because it is making you feel uncomfortable. If Ray suddenly plays dumb and claims, "I don't know what you're talking about," be prepared to explain when and under what circumstances this has happened before.

Should Ray continue this behavior, keep a journal or diary documenting exactly what happened and how you responded. Advise the other women to do the same, so you can support your complaints.

If Ray still doesn't behave properly even after you have shown that you have all found his behavior objectionable and have asked him to stop, go to Ray's supervisor to lodge your complaints, preferably as a group. Then, with group involvement and documentation, you have more than a she said/he said situation and your complaint is likely to be addressed. Both Ray and his supervisor have been put on notice about his offensive behavior, which could lead to a successful suit against the company as well as Ray for sexual harassment and for creating a hostile workplace environment. Either of these claims could mean a big bucks payout for the organization, along with some bad press.

Don't fan the flames by fighting Ray on his level. Staring at him the way he stares at you is likely to backfire rather than make a point. In fact, Ray might enjoy the attention or getting a rise out of you, even if you and the other women employees are laughing at him. He could think of your response as a big joke and might enjoy the feeling that he is getting to you and the other women. Plus, if you and the other women are responding in kind, you defeat your chances of making a case that you find his behavior offensive and harassing, since he might argue you are all just playing a fun office game. The call from a friend in the media possibly might work to let Ray know that continuing his offensive behavior could gain public attention. This approach could put a quick stop to his ardent staring, too.

In short, speak up to stop the behavior sooner rather than later. If a first complaint to another level doesn't work, try again. Keep records of what he Ray has done and when, and be ready to go formal with your complaint if your second effort doesn't prevail.

Today's Take-Aways

☑ If your boss is looking in all the wrong places, give him clear directions to look another way.

☑ Just as traffic going the wrong way needs a sign to change direction, so does a boss who is looking and behaving in the wrong way. Pull out your stop sign to remind him to stop and take another route.

☑ If you feel your boss is out of line with lascivious looks and lewd behavior, it's time to pull in the rope and get him in line. Speak up and let him know you're about to pull on that rope.

☑ If at first you don't succeed when you complain about a boss who's out of line, complain, complain again—first to the boss and then to others.

☑ Don't give an out-of-line boss more slack; instead, stand up to him and cut the line.

A New Boss Is Insulting and Abusive

When a new boss takes over an office, sometimes it can spell trouble for the people already there. The problem for employees is that you have already developed a bond with the boss who has left and that boss has created a cultural climate to which people have generally adapted. You know the rules and you know where you stand. A new boss may have new ways of doing things which can create problems for employees who are used to things being a certain way. A new boss may also feel she has to be particularly tough in asserting authority or risk having that authority undermined. As a result, any employee who stands up can be perceived as a threat. Employees who don't quickly adapt to the new regime and its expectations can be seen as impediments to the new boss successfully taking charge. The result can be a supercritical, even hostile, boss who puts you on edge.

That's what happened to Evelyn, then in her twenties, when she was first placed by a temporary agency on a production job for a large office supply store. After a few weeks, the job became permanent. A few weeks after that, Evelyn's supervisor was promoted to another store branch, and a new boss, Justine, took over. Justine inherited the small production team that was already in place at the store, and that's when the problems developed. According to Evelyn, Justine spoke to the staff members in a "derogatory" way from the start.

"She was just insulting and out of line. She would tell me, 'A monkey could do your job. I don't see how you were hired.' She thought I was incapable of doing the filing and typing to her satisfaction, and she would rake me over the coals."

Evelyn also noted that Justine engaged in the same insulting behavior toward another woman, June. June was a quiet, unassertive Asian woman who was brought in to learn the business by a relative. Justine was highly critical of June, telling her, "You're slow and stupid, and just because your father works in another department of the company, don't think you can get special privileges." Her tirade reduced June to tears, but June just meekly said she would try to do better, and the incident blew over.

As Justine continued to rule the roost and pick on the underlings, the employees' response was to mainly commiserate among each other. For a time, Evelyn continued to back down like the others, apologizing and saying she would try to do better whenever Justine hurled out insults at her.

The problem heated up when another employee went on maternity leave and Justine asked Evelyn to take on some of the woman's work, which included acting as a receptionist and handling customer calls and complaints. This gave Justine even more things to criticize about Evelyn. At the same time, she continued her insulting comments to others. As Evelyn put it:

> *Justine would show me and other people how to do a job. Then, when we made the slightest mistake, like forgetting to have the printer warmed up right away when we had files to print, she would say, "You're stupid," or "You didn't follow my instructions correctly." One time, she even grabbed the paper from my hands to teach me how to collate, though I knew how to do something as simple as that. She also told me one time, "You make everyone uncomfortable." So nobody liked Justine because of the way she treated everybody, and when she wasn't around, the production process went just fine without her.*

Still, Evelyn remained at the job for another three months, though the insults and derogatory remarks continued. Finally, things boiled over when Evelyn put some positive affirmation signs on her desk. The signs were meant to function as friendly, positive affirmations, but Justine insisted that Evelyn get rid of them. When Evelyn tried to protest, saying they were just nice supportive comments, Justine responded angrily, telling her, "You're pushing your beliefs on other people." This time, when Evelyn tried to explain, Justine fired her on the spot.

What Should Evelyn Have Done?

Is there anything Evelyn might have done differently or did she make the best choice at the time? In Evelyn's place, what would you do and why? What do you think the outcomes of these different options would be? Here are some possibilities:

➲ Don't put up with verbal abuse. Ask Justine right away for time to talk about what's wrong so you can do a better job and stop the abuse.

➲ Recognize that Justine is probably acting in this supercritical way because she has taken over the staff from someone else, feels insecure, and wants to show her authority. That way you won't take the abuse personally.

➲ Talk to June and others who have experienced verbal abuse and set up a meeting to talk to Justine together.

➲ Send Justine a memo documenting the times when she has verbally abused you or unreasonably told you what to do, such as telling you to take positive sayings off your desk. Tell her that you are hoping for change, so you'd like to discuss these issues. The underlying threat is that you have documented the abuse, so she better listen or else!

➲ Take a stand as soon as Justine starts to put you down, but do so gently and diplomatically so Justine doesn't feel threatened.

➲ Organize a welcome party for Justine with others on the staff so she feels more secure and will become more friendly to others.

➲ Notice the times when Justine tends to get verbally abusive to you and ask her how you can do a better job. Ask if she can give you written rather than verbal instructions.

In this case, multiple strategies might work well, since there is no one easy way to deal with a new boss who is defensive and abusive.

It's possible that a major factor triggering Justine's overly aggressive behavior is that she not only is new, but also has inherited a staff. Thus, Justine is already feeling insecure and under great pressure, which could well be why she cracks down on anything that seems ineffective, inefficient, or distracting, e.g., putting positive affirmations on a desk.

Given this possible underlying dynamic driving her abusive behavior, you might do well to take some action with the other employees to welcome Justine and make her feel immediately more at home and supported by staff. For example, the group might organize a welcome party. Another good first step is to set up a meeting to discuss what everyone is doing and what procedures and policies Justine would like everyone to follow. As an alternative, ask to meet with Justine soon after she has criticized you once or twice for doing something wrong. This way, you will have a better idea of what Justine wants and you will show her that you really want to do a good job. You'll also show her you are not going to retreat in the face of insults or putdowns, but want to deal with the problem now so you can be more productive in the future. Don't be confrontational in any of these meetings, as this could lead Justine to feel even more under attack and defensive as the new boss in town. As long as you are diplomatic and empathetic, Justine is apt to respond in kind to deal with the problem rather than defending against it.

It might also be a good idea to start documenting any abusive behavior aimed at you and others just in case. Keep this to yourself initially. At this stage, it's better not to show you are keeping copious notes since this might make Justine more defensive. Documenting problems can make someone in authority think you are contemplating litigation. Although that might be a possibility, it should be a remote one since it's best to resolve any problems with your boss directly. When a boss is new and hasn't had time to build up a reputation with others in the organization or gain the confidence of employees in the management role, she may welcome the opportunity to work through any problems.

So think of how to deal with the underlying dynamics causing the boss to behave badly, Then, you can better know how to approach the situation. With awareness and understanding of the problem comes insight on how to solve it.

Today's Take-Aways

☑ When a new boss is overly aggressive and abusive, it may due to insecurity. If so, you'll go much further by helping the boss feel secure, not by shutting down or going on the attack.

☑ A good way to stand up to a boss who's being abusive—or to anyone for that matter—is to sit down to talk about it.

☑ To get off the ropes with a new boss, trying showing your boss the ropes.

25

Call 911

What do you do if your boss has a serious drug or alcohol problem? An addiction can manifest itself in various ways, from extreme irritability, to lapses of memory, to physical breakdowns. And sometimes the cost of a habit can lead to criminal behavior, such as embezzling money or stealing property from the company to support the habit. In a large company, this problem might be more easily resolved, since once the boss's supervisors or top executives learn what is going on, they'll deal with the situation right away. For example, they might require the boss to participate in a rehab program. In such a case, employees might do well to notify higher-ups if the addictive behavior continues and let them handle the situation, perhaps by terminating the boss's employment. But this kind of problem can be more complicated in a smaller company where the boss is heading the company, leaving employees uncertain of what to do since there is no one to appeal to above the boss.

That's the problem Alex faced when he got a job doing accounting for a small parts distributor with a dozen employees headed by Rosalind and her husband, George. George primarily handled the sales and spent much of his time away from the office, while Rosalind managed the office. At first, everything seemed fine, and Alex and the other employees liked the homey, family feeling of the small company.

But then Rosalind had a seizure in the office after overdosing on prescription dugs. It was like epilepsy, Alex recalled. "We were all pretty scared," he said. "She was in another room when it started, and we heard this squealing noise. Then she went into convulsions." Since the small town where the company was located didn't have a 911 emergency dispatch to call, the staff members put the boss in the back of a pick-up truck and drove her around the corner to the hospital while she was still convulsing. Fortunately, the hospital staff was able to treat her, and after a few days she returned to work.

However, the problem continued because Rosalind was addicted to prescription drugs. This addiction not only led to another seizure a few months later, but other conflicts arose in the office due to the effects of the drugs. For example, Rosalind hid money in the office on several occasions that she and George were going to use for one of their frequent weekend trips. But when she didn't remember where she put it, she would accuse George or the employees of stealing it.

The employees generally dealt with Rosalind's problem by doing their jobs as best they could and "keeping out of her way," though resentment built because Rosalind and George took a lot of money out of the company to support a fancy lifestyle with expensive cars but asked the employees to take pay cuts.

Finally, after months of escalating tension, Rosalind went into rehab for several weeks, and Alex had to figure out how to do her job while she was gone. He asked George for a pay increase, which he got, but when Rosalind returned, she was angry about the raise. When Alex came to the office wearing a new suit one day, she glared at him, making him feel very uncomfortable, though he said nothing. Even more odd behavior followed, due to the other drugs she was taking. While her husband told all the doctors in town not to prescribe any drugs for her, Alex reported that didn't solve the problem. "She started taking Ravenol instead, and she used to walk around the office with her jeans zipper undone, telling everyone how she hadn't s**t in a week, due to the drug," Alex said. "So it was really uncomfortable in the office."

What Should Alex Do?

In Alex's place, what would you do and why? What do you think the outcomes of these different options would be? Here are some possibilities:

➲ Try not to take Rosalind's odd behavior personally. Her drug problem has nothing to do with you.

➲ As best you can, do Rosalind's job when she isn't able to do it herself.

➲ Ask Rosalind and George for a promotion and another raise, since you are doing more responsible work because of Rosalind's problems.

➲ Tell Rosalind when you feel her behavior is offensive and urge the other employees to do the same. If enough of you say something, she will clean up her act.

➲ Tell George when Rosalind is out of line so he will understand he needs to get her additional help.

➲ Start preparing your resume, and look for a drug-free workplace.

Probably a combination of strategies would work best here. A big obstacle to making any changes in this case is that Rosalind and George own the company so there are no higher-ups to whom to appeal. In a larger company, someone with Rosalind's drug problem would either have to complete rehab successfully or be fired. But here Rosalind is still having drug problems, though now with different drugs. So the best recourse is to make the best of a bad situation as long as you stay, while looking into other job possibilities if things don't improve.

When dealing with a person who has personality and behavioral problems due to drugs, a good approach is to work on detaching yourself from the situation so you don't take the behavior personally. Consider their actions to be "the drugs talking," rather than taking offense at their odd behaviors and reactions. As much as you are able, take over the work they are unable to do, but seek extra recognition and compensation for this. After all, if you are doing more responsible work, a promotion and new title might be in order, and that will help down the road when you are seeking your next job.

Possibly, too, join with the other employees to keep Rosalind's husband informed of what's going on at work. Since he is often on the road selling the company's services, he may not be fully aware of the continuing problem and, as her husband, he may be in a better position to do something about it. Perhaps, too, you and the other employees might find ways to show sympathy and support to Rosalind, which might give her more strength to fight her addiction.

Friendly gestures such as putting on a surprise party for Rosalind to welcome her back after a trip or after she has taken some time out for drug treatment might help her deal with her problem and lead to a better work environment for everyone.

Today's Take-Aways

☑ If your boss has a drug problem, remember that sometimes the odd behavior is due to the "drugs talking," and it may keep things running more smoothly if you don't take it personally.

☑ If you have to do more work to cover for a boss with a drug problem, it may be time for a raise and/or promotion to compensate for that extra work.

☑ Sometimes a boss with an addiction problem may need more help than you can give; if so, it may be time to get out.

26

Drunk, Disorderly, and Untouchable

When a boss has a drinking problem and becomes abusive, the situation generally is taken care of once top management finds out about it. The boss is told to shape up or ship out, and sometimes she is sent off for some management training and shown ways to better relate to employees. The problem is solved.

But what happens if the boss's immediate supervisor doesn't want to do anything because she is trying to protect the boss for some reason. Perhaps there is a personal connection, or perhaps the boss may have some damaging information about the supervisor. The source of appeal may be cut off, particularly if top management takes a hands-off approach or is located in another city, state, or country. In such a case, when employees stay on for whatever reason, a major source of support may be commiserating with each other because dealing with the boss seems so grim and demoralizing. They fear doing anything that might rock the boat, even though some gentle rocking may be exactly what is needed.

That's what happened to Kevin when he got a job as a reporter at the headquarters of a chain newspaper. In many ways, it was a dream job. The work was different each day, and Kevin enjoyed covering the latest news and meeting interesting people while on assignment. Plus, times were tough, so Kevin felt fortunate to have a job at all in this highly competitive field.

Yet Kevin and about fifty other employees felt used and abused working for Nanette, who had been promoted to assignment editor after proving herself as a cracker-jack reporter for several years. Among the complaints that Kevin and the other employees had was that Nanette had a drinking problem. She was often insulting and demeaning, usually berating people by phone or e-mail, whether they were located in the main office or in one of the paper's many branches around the United States.

Nanette's problem behavior was not only common but often observable. For example, she would show up at press conferences and conventions soused and become loud and obnoxious. In one case, she went out to dinner with a big group of employees and clients and ran up a $400 tab of food and drinks, but gave the waiter a very small tip. When the hotel manager and waiter came after her to complain, she loudly argued back, "Do you know who I am?" and stormed out without paying the waiter anything more.

Kevin described the e-mails that Nanette would frequently send to him and other employees as insulting. They would say things like, "Get a clue," or "You really dropped the ball," or "Why wasn't this done?" She never offered any praise or pointed up the reporter's strong points. Instead, she was always tearing everyone down. In one case, she even sent an e-mail to everyone in the office disparaging one employee and included that employee on the distribution list "by mistake."

Making matters worse, she routinely gave out too many assignments to each employee, so they often required lots of overtime. The employees typically worked 14 hours a day, from about 7 a.m. to 8 p.m.

But when some employees complained to Nanette's immediate supervisor, he didn't do anything. Why not? Some employees soon discovered the reason through the office grapevine. Nanette apparently had some information she could use against her supervisor if he ever tried to discipline her. A married man, the supervisor apparently had had an affair with an employee and was terrified that Nanette might tell his wife. As a result, when several employees came to him to complain about Nanette, he was very protective of her, telling them that she really needed this job and that she had been a good reporter. Nothing was done to address the problem.

Thus, without anyone in management to back them up, Kevin

and the other employees generally just grumbled among themselves, either face-to-face if they worked in the same office or by phone if they worked in different offices. Occasionally, an employee would get up the nerve to stand up to Nanette, but those exceptions were few and far between. Most of the employees felt cowed and power-less in the face of Nanette's abuse, especially knowing her supervisor would protect her at any cost, and that they faced a very tight job market if they were to leave.

Kevin's response to this situation was to become a workaholic, neglecting himself and others to dedicate himself to the job. His long hours were increasingly causing conflicts with his wife at home. He didn't feel in a position to leave, yet he needed to do something.

What Should Kevin Do?

In Kevin's place, what would you do and why? What do you think the outcomes of these different options would be? Here are some possibilities:

- ⮑ Even if it seems scary to do so, speak to other employees about organizing a group meeting with Nanette either in person or via speakerphone.

- ⮑ Talk to Nanette's supervisor and explain the problem with Nanette. If the supervisor once again comes to her aid, point out that you and the other employees already know about his affair with another employee.

- ⮑ Set up a meeting with Nanette and explain that you want to do a good job, but the pressure is interfering with your home and family life. Tell her you want to work out some way that you can reduce your hours to about 50–60 a week instead of 90.

- ⮑ Learn to stand up to Nanette and say no when she wants to give you too many assignments to handle, explaining that you want to do a good job on the assignments you already have.

- ⮑ Arrange with your wife to call in a family emergency from time to time so you can get some much needed time off.

- ⮑ Find a way to tune out Nanette's insulting e-mails and phone calls so you don't feel so stressed. Try turning your attention elsewhere or putting on some relaxing music in your office.

➲ Send an anonymous e-mail to the top management to let them know that the employees are finding it difficult to work with Nanette and suggest that she might benefit from a management training program.

Part of the problem here may be that Nanette lacks management skills. She was promoted into management after being a good reporter, but being a manager requires different skills from being an editor, skills such as motivating and supporting employees rather than tearing them down. Nanette's drinking problem is also contributing to the problem, as is the support she is getting from her immediate supervisor. Since she has information about him that can hurt him, she is in essence blackmailing him to support her in return for her not saying anything about his affair to his wife.

Given that this problem is affecting all of the employees, an initial strategy should be to try to gain support from other employees and presenting a united front. So far, Nanette has been able to cow everybody through fear of being fired. However, if you and other employees can break through your fear and start organizing as a group, you may find there is strength in numbers. Once a few of you make the break, it seems likely that others will come forward. Consider Nanette to be like the drug dealer or gang leader on the block who is ruling the neighborhood through intimidation. When a group of neighbors start to speak out, others will come to their aid, and the neighbors begin to take back control of their block. So you are a little like the block captain who is getting a team of people together to take back control of your life.

Secondly, just as the intimidated neighbors can use some help to deal with the problem—in their case from the beat cop—so might you and your group look for outside support. Nanette's supervisor might have turned down individual requests to stop the abuse, but a group meeting with him could have more influence, particularly if you can produce e-mails or reports of phone conversations showing the extent of her abuse. Perhaps you could let the supervisor know that you and others in the office already know about the problem she is holding over his head and you consider it a personal matter.

Finally, be prepared to say no to Nanette diplomatically when she makes unreasonable demands, and encourage other employees to do the same. Explain that you need to do this so you can continue to do a quality job on the assignments you currently have and not shortchange them or burn out yourself due to overwork and stress. In other words, show the boss how she will benefit in the long run by acting more reasonably toward you in the work she assigns. As others demand the same better treatment and respect, she will realize she has to change herself or risk losing good employees because she is demanding too much. Top management, even if they are hands-off or located elsewhere, will notice if good employees start to leave. Yes, it may be a tight job situation out there, but it's tight for Nanette, too. As she sees her employees taking more power and finds that her effort to control by blackmailing her supervisor is over, she will realize her own job could be at risk if she doesn't change.

Today's Take-Aways

☑ If you're feeling powerless, take back your power to gain empowerment—and take it from your boss.

☑ Don't feel cowed by your boss. Instead, join with other employees and become a herd so you can get heard.

☑ Taking back your job from a power-hungry, abusive boss is like taking back a neighborhood from drug dealers and gang leaders. You've got to join together and stand up to your boss as a group or you'll continue to fall down on your own.

☑ When you feel someone is driving over you, you need the drive to stop them by taking a different route.

The Intrusive Boss

Even in today's privacy-conscious society, it is still generally accepted that employers can pretty much monitor whatever activities they want that are done with their equipment or occur on their premises. They can also monitor employees who are working out in the field, such as salespeople or researchers. The usual policy is to let employees know the scope of what employers are monitoring, which helps to make employees feel more comfortable. They may not like this monitoring and may prefer that they aren't being observed, but at least they know the ground rules. It's not only legal for employers to observe, but it makes sense. Employers are generally liable for what employees do when they make mistakes, and it seems fair to know if employees are using their employer's time or property for personal matters.

But what if the monitoring goes beyond such guidelines, to the point that you feel your boss is intruding into your personal life or expecting too much of you after hours? You may feel the boss is being too nosy or controlling, trying to control and manage you from beyond the office. The problem is setting boundaries and developing techniques to set these boundaries more firmly to keep the boss from breaking in. You may want to consider moving your boundaries a little further out, or you may have to learn to accept the boundary-busting if you want to remain comfortably on the job. In some cases, the intrusive boss can get this way because you have a personal, off-the-job relationship, but that's another story.

Dealing with an intrusive boss is what Margie experienced in her work as a sales rep for a manufacturing company. Her job consisted of making sales calls to corporations, writing up reports, setting up and running a company table at occasional conferences, and going to sales and incentive meetings. At first, she liked the job, and she liked her friendly, chatty boss, Veronica, who owned the company. But after a few weeks, Veronica became more and more intrusive. Initially, when Margie went to a business sales conference to learn new sales techniques, she thought it reasonable, albeit a bit disruptive, for Veronica to ask her to call in each morning she was at the conference and then again at the end of the day. Margie had to pull herself away from meetings to make these calls, but still did so willingly.

However, it got worse when Veronica began to insist that Margie call in anytime she was out of the office, including when she was on vacation or sick. Margie wasn't unique in this regard; Veronica required the other employees to call in as well. Soon, Margie began to think of Veronica as a "tyrant with a capital *T*", and she even dubbed Veronica "the Psycho Hose Beast," since she came to think of her as an obsessive-compulsive woman who had to know and control everything, and who sucked her dry in the process. As Margie commented in an e-mail:

> *The woman who shall hereafter be referred to as the Psycho Hose Beast insisted that I call in whenever I was out of the office. This wouldn't be bad except that I didn't just have to do it when I was traveling on business, but also when I was out sick or on vacation. Even one day when I was out with a dreaded throwing-up disease, she wanted me to take the phone with me into the toilet, so I could return my calls.*

> *The worst was when I was expected to call in and check my messages during my honeymoon. I called in and was told in dire tones that the Psycho Hose Beast wanted to speak to me immediately. So I waited on the phone until she came on, and immediately, she began lamenting that my desk was piled high with work and I had a ton of it to do and I was falling very far behind.*

Margie became so frustrated at the interruption to her honeymoon, that as Veronica ranted on, she hung up and didn't call back the rest of the time she was gone. She felt safe from Veronica's intrusiveness since she hadn't left the number of the hotel or told her where she would be. When she returned from her honeymoon, Veronica didn't say anything about the aborted communication, although she continued to demand that Margie call in as she had before.

Additionally, Margie felt Veronica intruded on her personal space in turning some of her break time during the day into company time. "Veronica used our lunch break as time for a staff meeting," Margie complained. "We were not allowed to mark the lunch time as billable time to the company because it was considered our 'personal lunch time.' And if we used our cars to do any business for the company, she wouldn't let us request a reimbursement, saying this was just a 'discretionary' expense." Repeatedly, Veronica found ways to intrude on Margie's and other employees' personal time, but they were never compensated.

What Should Margie Have Done?

Is there anything Margie might have done differently to ward off her overly intrusive boss? In Margie's place, what would you do and why? What do you think the outcomes of these different options would be? Here are some possibilities:

- ⤷ Turn off the phone when you are on vacation or sick so Veronica can't reach you.

- ⤷ Tell Veronica your car isn't available for doing company business unless you are compensated for using it, and blame the change on your accountant or husband.

- ⤷ Don't return your messages right away when Veronica calls you at home so she gets the message and stops calling you when you are away from work.

- ⤷ Talk to the other employees about how Veronica has been turning your personal time into work time without compensation. Then, as a group, ask Veronica to set up the staff meetings during the work day, not at lunch.

- ⤷ If Veronica turns some of your personal time into work time, take some time for yourself during the work day in exchange. It's only fair.

➲ Set up a meeting with Veronica in which you diplomatically explain how you need for your personal time to be your personal time and that you are respectfully asking her to honor that.

➲ Set up a meeting with Veronica and the other employees in which you all ask Veronica to respect your personal time by not calling you when you're off work. Ask that she compensate you when you use your lunch breaks or your own cars for company business.

In this case, Veronica is going beyond the boundaries of what is normally acceptable by intruding on your private life and personal time at work. However, she is the owner of the company and the situation has been going on for some time, not just with you but with other employees. Thus, once a pattern has been set up, it can be difficult to make changes to reclaim that personal space. Perhaps you could try gradually reclaiming your space individually or as a group of employees in various ways. Notice what works, continue to do that, and drop the other strategies that aren't working.

A good way to analyze the situation and decide what to do is to think about why Veronica is making these intrusions. Is it because she is unsure whether you or others have done or will do certain work and is riding you so closely so she can double-check? If so, take some company time to write up in more detail what you have done or plan to do and leave it with her. In other words, anticipate her reasons for calling you when you are off the job and address these to make her feel more secure so she won't need to call you for that reason.

Another possible reason that Veronica is intruding is because she enjoys the feeling of power and control. It is like a game to prove that she is in charge and can tell you and the others what to do. In that case, treat her calls more like a game and prevent her from playing you. For example, don't be available when she calls and have her calls picked up by an answering machine or a family member. This way, you can conveniently be out for the evening, away for the weekend, or unreachable until very late, and the best she can do is leave a message for you. Then, if she leaves a message for you to call back, you might delay the return call. If she emphasizes how urgent it is to contact you, try calling back very late. In other words, find ways to make it less desirable for her to call you and interrupt your vacations, personal time or sick days.

Another possibility is for you individually or with a group of employees to set up a meeting with Veronica to explain in a very diplomatic way that you would like to discuss something that is causing stress and a loss of productivity. When you do have this discussion, point up how this change can help her company do better. This will give Veronica an incentive to change an ingrained pattern that has been working for her so far. Then, talk about how you would like to work out some understandings about when you have personal time and when you feel it is fair that you get reimbursed when you use your own equipment on the job.

Think of this meeting as a chance to clarify and modify the boundaries between work and personal space. Have a goal in mind, but be willing to make compromises as you negotiate what those boundaries should be. For example, maybe Veronica would be willing to pay you more for work when she holds a staff meeting during your lunch hour, or compensate you for using your car for company business. Sometimes by making it clear what these boundaries are, you are in a better position to negotiate changes, particularly if you can do this as a group. As a sole proprietor, Veronica may not want to risk losing her whole staff and so may be more open to compromise when legally she is in the wrong.

In sum, try out different strategies based on what you think Veronica's main motives are for intruding on your personal space and time. Then, with some insight into these motives, you can better determine the best incentives for change. Or gradually change your own behavior to indicate what is acceptable and what isn't, since that might subtly influence Veronica to change. Of course, you always have the alternative of accepting the way things are if you like the job enough to stay, and then you can find ways to relax and better accept the status quo. But first, strive for change.

Today's Take-Aways

- ☑ If your boss is invading your personal space, it's time to set up some boundaries.
- ☑ Depending on the situation, think of resetting the boundaries as more of a straightforward negotiation or a hide-and-seek game with a boss who is trying to find you when you don't want to be found.
- ☑ If your boss is being too nosy, think about different ways to keep her from picking up your scent.

28

Party Planner

What could possibly be bad about a boss who wants his employees to have fun? A party attitude may seem harmless—even a great benefit—on the surface, but it can become a problem if the boss wants employees to participate in after-hours entertainment and gets mad at employees who don't want to participate. Even if the employee has a good reason for not joining in, such as family obligations, it doesn't matter to the party boss. This boss is looking for employees who want to have fun when the workday is over. While those who do join in may enjoy the party and the perks, those who don't may feel cut off and disadvantaged when it comes time to work.

That's the situation faced by Patricia, then in her late twenties, when she began working for a company in the fashion industry. Her boss, Gary, was a single man in his late forties or early fifties. Once or twice a week, he liked to go out to the local night clubs after work until closing time, and he extended invitations to the half dozen women on his staff to join him. The five other women in the office were also in their early twenties, and they jumped at the chance to enjoy the party scene on the boss's dime, since Gary paid for everyone. However, Patricia had a husband and two young children, so she respectfully declined to go, explaining she had to be home with her family.

The first few times she declined, everything seemed fine. Gary just said, "Sorry you won't be joining us," and that was the end of it. But after the fourth or fifth time, she found that Gary would stop talking to her at the office for the next few days afterward. He seemed to look straight through her if they passed in the hall, and if she came to his office to ask him something, he brusquely waved her off without saying anything. Then he would talk to her for a few days, but shut her off again after she turned down the next invitation.

Patricia tried to talk to Gary a few times about the problem, once on an evening when they were both working late and another time at an office party at a local bar. When she approached Gary at the office, he was short with her. "I can't talk about this now," he told her. "I'm too busy." And when she spoke to him at the bar, telling him she hoped to clear up any misunderstanding, he looked annoyed and said, "No, I don't want to talk about this at work." So Patricia felt she couldn't discuss the situation with Gary, and when she spoke to his supervisor, he simply told her there was nothing that could be done. "That's the way Gary is," the supervisor said. "You just have to learn to deal with it." Eventually, Patricia felt so frustrated and uncomfortable around Gary, not to mention afraid that any day she might be fired, that she left the company and the industry for a while, even though she loved the work.

When I spoke to her, she said she thought maybe Gary behaved this way because going to the parties with his staff members made him feel important. Since he was an older single man without a girlfriend, maybe this was his way to "get a life," because "his work was his life." She said maybe he felt angry at her for not going along with the others after work, for not being part of his "fun group." Now, looking back, Patricia thought if she had it to do over, she might have tried to make some arrangements with her husband that would have allowed her to go out occasionally. "I might have done more to be part of Gary's Gang, even if this really wasn't part of my job, and maybe that might have made him feel better about me," she said.

What Should Patricia Have Done?

Is there anything Patricia might have done differently? In Patricia's place, what would you do and why? What do you think the outcomes of these different options would be? Here are some possibilities:

⮺ Plan to go to the parties with the group about once a week, and find a babysitter to take care of the kids at home.

⮺ Go to the parties for about a half an hour or so after work, and then find a way to gracefully leave early.

⮺ Since Gary won't talk to you, send him a memo explaining that you can't go because you have to be home with your husband and kids, not because you don't want to go to the clubs with him and the others.

⮺ Do a good job at work and don't worry about it when Gary won't talk to you after you have turned down one of his invitations. That's just his way, and he hasn't tried to fire you in the past.

⮺ Find some other way to show you appreciate Gary in order to break through his stony silences. Show him, too, how important your family is to you, perhaps by bringing him a cake from a family gathering.

In this case, Gary's requests for Patricia to attend these after-work parties are beyond the scope of the job and his silence for several days after Patricia's refusals are unsettling and immature. Like a child who can't get what he wants from his parents, he retreats to his room and sulks for awhile. But at least he is not requiring anything more than the attendance of his staffers as a group; he is not trying to hit on or date anyone, and his own supervisor just feels he is being eccentric. Moreover, Gary seems to be using these events to create a fun, family-like setting with others at work, perhaps because he is so into his work that he has little or no outside social life.

Since you like the job, and since Gary is unlikely to change and the other employees who participate in these parties enjoy it, you might consider ways you can adapt to create a compromise situation. For example, you might talk to your husband about working out some arrangements where once a week you can attend these after-hours outings. Another solution might be to go the parties when asked, but plan to leave after an hour or two rather than staying until closing time like the others do. Or perhaps a combination of going occasionally and leaving earlier from time to time might work.

In addition, you might combine going to the clubs occasionally with some gesture of appreciation, such as bringing in a cake from a family event to help Gary and others in the office appreciate better your need to spend time with your family.

In short, though technically Gary's expectations for off-the-job partying are beyond the requirements for the job, you might still find a way to compromise to better balance his desire to have you participate along with others in the group with your desire to be there for your family. In effect, Gary has created a party-fun culture in the organization, which he has been trying to maintain, and by not participating at all, you are the odd person out in the company. To you, Gary may be a bad boss for expecting you to participate in extracurricular activities and then ignoring or avoiding you in the office to show his displeasure. But for those who like these activities, he's not a bad boss at all.

Today's Take-Aways

- ☑ Sometimes the bad boss is in the eye of the beholder; one person's bad boss may be another person's dream boss.

- ☑ If the boss wants you to join the party, consider becoming part of the party line.

- ☑ If your boss's style isn't to your taste, try a little seasoning to improve it.

- ☑ Sometimes a boss just seems bad because you aren't part of the "in" crowd or office culture; if that is true for you, think of ways to build a bridge to the other side.

29 Cultural Divide

Sometimes cultural differences can contribute to problems in the workplace. A boss's behavior may be unacceptable to employees though the boss sees no problem with it because it is accepted in his or her culture. In larger companies, cultural diversity training has become a recent addition to many employee and manager training programs. When there's a cultural divide in the workplace, employee complaints and management education may help to overcome the differences and indicate what behavior is acceptable. But what if the boss is the owner of a smaller business without these supports in place? In this case, it may be more difficult to let the boss know anything is wrong. Still, some discussion and cultural education might still be a way to seek change, as opposed to quitting in disgust or frustration.

That's the situation Julie encountered when she worked as a waitress in a Korean restaurant while between administrative jobs. Her boss, Ron, was a forty-five-year-old man from Korea. Ron thought it amusing—and perfectly acceptable—to smack the women who worked for him playfully on the backside and make humorous sexual comments such as "Nice butt." He didn't try to date or hit on any of the women because he was married, and his wife and children were at the restaurant most of the time. But when they went out for a short time, he would go around inappropriately patting the women and making the remarks as if he had been suddenly freed from ordinary proprieties because his wife was away.

Julie and the other women in the restaurant—several other waitresses and two cooks—tried to ignore his words and actions, but Julie felt continually steamed and demeaned by them. Finally, after three months, she quit without confronting either Ron or his wife about exactly what was wrong. "I did stick it out for three months, but that was all that I could handle," she explained to me. "I told his wife that I was tired of the unwanted advances of 'certain people' in the restaurant and I walked out." But was that really the best way to deal with the situation?

What Should Julie Have Done?

Is there anything Julie might have done differently or should do if she has such a boss in the future? In Julie's place, what would you do and why? What do you think the outcomes of these different options would be? Here are some possibilities:

- ➲ Tell Ron you don't like being slapped on the butt, don't like the racy comments, and ask him to stop.

- ➲ Talk to the other women who similarly object to Ron's behavior and then confront him as a group. There's strength in numbers and you are less likely to lose your jobs if you go to him together.

- ➲ Tell Ron's wife early on what he has been doing. Ask her to talk to her husband and ask him to stop.

- ➲ Recognize that Ron is behaving this way because it is acceptable in his culture and don't let his rude behavior and remarks upset you. Just ignore them like nothing has happened.

- ➲ Wear a buzzer in your pants so the next time Ron hits you inappropriately, he'll get a big shock and get the idea.

- ➲ If Ron doesn't stop, threaten that you and the other women will report him to the authorities who regulate restaurants. That should get his attention.

While Ron's behavior is unacceptable to you and the other women and would normally be considered harassment, there's no supervisor or top executives to complain to because Ron owns the business.

Plus, he's from another culture where this kind of behavior toward female employees is not considered wrong. By his standards, he's just being playful and making sexual jibes to titillate while his wife and children are not very far away. This kind of behavior would be winked at for men in his position in his home country.

Rather than remaining quiet and simply quitting when you can't take it anymore, a better approach would be to speak to Ron, either individually or as a group of women. Tell him diplomatically that he is making you feel uncomfortable with his actions. While he may think what he is doing is humorous and playful, explain that you are all upset by it and would like him to stop.

Such a frank talk might do the trick, and if not, a next step might be to talk to his wife when she is at the restaurant. Perhaps a way to do this and still help Ron save face (which is especially important in Asian cultures) is to approach his wife and ask to speak to her confidentially about something that has been bothering you. When you talk to her, you can let her know that other women feel the same way, and ask if she can do anything to intercede with her husband to get him to stop. If Ron won't listen to you or the other women individually or as a group, he might change if he realizes that you have spoken to his wife. She then knows what he has been doing, and he realizes that she is in your corner in making her request on your behalf.

If Ron still doesn't stop, well, maybe that's the time to leave if his behavior is still bothering you. Otherwise, chalk up the situation to cultural misunderstandings and perhaps think of Ron as a middle-aged married man just letting off a little steam by engaging in behavior that is acceptable in his culture. Besides, it's probably pretty harmless, since his wife and children are around the restaurant most of the time.

Today's Take-Aways

☑ If the problem with your boss is rooted in cultural differences, try using cultural education to reduce those differences.

☑ If you're steaming because your boss is doing something you think he shouldn't, try letting the steam off by telling him what he's doing wrong.

☑ If you want your boss to stop doing something, tell him directly rather than hoping he'll be able to read your "stop" signs.

☑ When there's a cultural divide, try speaking up to bridge those differences before they increase and multiply.

Part V

Ethical Challenges

30 Dealing with Danger

It might make sense to go along with a very difficult, demanding, disrespectful boss in a highly competitive industry, especially when that's the main route to getting ahead. However, it may not be the best strategy when an ongoing abusive situation turns into a dangerous one for yourself or others. For a time, monitoring a deteriorating situation might work when that's the norm of doing business in the industry. But when deterioration turns into an immediate threat, it may time for you or someone with more power to take some action. After all, if you're assisting someone who creates a dangerous condition, you share some of the responsibility, and you might be found liable or guilty of a crime. It's like you're being asked to give someone a rope he might use to hang himself, or you're asked to lead someone to the edge of a cliff where he could fall off.

That's the situation Janice faced when she was working as an assistant for Derek, a director in the film industry. She had already come to terms with the unusually long hours and high level of stress working for demanding directors. But she was ready to speak up when Derek put two young children in danger because he was trying to get an early morning shot of them running down a steep hill that ended in a high cliff. She had already overlooked Derek's violation of industry guidelines that prohibited having young children on the set before 7 a.m. Derek had ignored those guidelines because he wanted the children on the set at 4 a.m. so he could shoot the scene at dawn, just as the sun was rising behind the hill. Even though the set had a designated representative from the welfare department to check that the children were being well treated, Derek was ready to ignore her, too.

Now danger loomed, as Janice got the children in place for their early morning run down the steep, rocky hillside. As she did so, the welfare worker approached Derek to tell him the shot was too dangerous. At the same time, the children began crying, afraid to do the run, and Derek called Janice on the radio, telling her to "get the welfare worker the f**k away from me."

Janice struggled with her own ethics as she went to talk to the welfare worker to persuade her not to interfere with the shot. On the one hand, Janice knew there were many different ways to get that shot, although she agreed with Derek that this particular shot would have the most impact for the moviegoers, demonstrating the sense of danger and fear necessary to the story. But at the same time, that feeling of danger and fear was all too real. Not only were the children crying hysterically, but the welfare worker was telling Janice that the planned action was much too dangerous and scary for the children. And Janice knew that she was right. Thus, she felt caught in the middle between the director's creative vision and escalating anger, her own fear the children could get hurt, and the welfare worker's warnings, which could turn into a lawsuit for damages.

In this case, Janice ultimately didn't have to do anything because Derek slipped on the rocky hillside and broke his ankle while screaming at Janice and the welfare worker to get the children in place for the shot. As he lay on the ground, writhing in pain and waiting for the ambulance to come take him to the hospital, Janice and the other crew members completed the rest of the shooting schedule and the shot that caused all the trouble had to be scrapped.

For Janice, this was a fortunate *deus ex machina* ending. She didn't have to compromise her own ethics, which she might have done in order to assure her job survival. As she later explained: "I never felt I had the strength as a woman in the industry to do anything since women are in such a weak position. There's so much sexism in the industry, though a lot more women have gained status in the last five years or so, much more so than when I was in the industry. So they now are at the level where they can say no. If I had said no, I know the director would have talked me into doing the shot, would have threatened me with penalties for insubordination, or would have fired me. And he could easily have done whatever he wanted, because film is a freelance industry where there is virtually no monitoring. Anything goes, even if it isn't legal."

Janice also explained that the ramifications of being fired from a job would have extended far beyond that job, since she would get a reputation of being uncooperative. She also felt that she would achieve the same result if she, as a Director's Guild member, asked for a field rep to come to monitor the set for a few days because of potentially dangerous conditions. "The director would soon learn it was me who called for the field rep, and I would get a bad reputation for that, too."

Janice was bothered that so many directors did go too far in endangering crew members and actors. So a year before she left the industry in frustration, she started a committee to promote greater awareness of safety and urge employees on the set to ask the Director's Guild to send in field reps to prevent directors from putting people in dangerous, life-threatening situations. "The industry will change if more people would stand up to the directors," she said. Though she had left the industry without doing this herself, she hoped others would do so, and she noted that there were already some positive changes, such as a requirement that if dangerous animals were on the set, someone must be around who could provide emergency care for an injury.

What Should Janice Have Done?

Is there anything Janice might have done differently? In Janice's place, what would you do and why? What do you think the outcomes of these different options would be? Here are some possibilities:

⊃ Quit before you engage in unethical or dangerous behavior that could kill or injure you or someone else on the set.

⊃ Quietly do your job, acknowledging that this is the way things are and that you don't have the power to change anything.

➲ Say nothing, hope for the best, and figure that the director's liability insurance will handle any claims for actors and crew members who get hurt.

➲ Contact others to discuss dangerous conditions on the set, and
  don't just talk about them; take a stand, such as refusing to
  order actors to do something that is very dangerous.

➲ Discuss the problems on the set with other staff members who
  feel as you do and ask the director as a group to make changes
  for everyone's safety.

➲ Talk to the director after the day's filming to discuss your concerns and urge him to make changes so you and others are safer.

➲ Complain to the Director's Guild if the director doesn't change
  his practices so the guild will put pressure on him to change.

Unfortunately, this situation is one of those cases where you can do
little to change the situation because you have very little power in
the industry you are in. The industry has developed a culture of risk,
which has become acceptable to industry professionals, despite legal,
health, and safety concerns. Many people outside the industry may
view the potential risks, particularly those which violate government
health and safety codes, as unacceptable in ethical or moral terms.
Yet this is how the industry operates, at least until further regulations and common practices are established. So in a sense, the "bad
boss" really reflects the norm in that industry.

   Thus, given the commonly accepted practices considered normal
and ethical in the industry, in the short term, you can do little more
than advise the director when a particular situation seems especially
dangerous or difficult to you. And given the way things work, you
have to defer to the director. Actively protesting or complaining to
the Director's Guild will be likely to get you fired or earn you the
reputation of being a difficult person to work with in the industry,
thus making it harder to get future jobs. Perhaps participating in or
organizing a small group whose goal is to achieve greater safety on
the set might be a way to work for long-term changes. But for the
current day-to-day job, you or anyone on the crew would generally
need to go along with what the director wants, even if it is personally
uncomfortable.

   As a result, the decision about what to do becomes more of a personal one. Based on an understanding the accepted culture of the industry, you must decide if its norms and standard are ones you feel comfortable with. In other words, even if certain practices by a boss seem wrong or overly dangerous to you, the question to ask yourself is: "Can I live in this kind of environment on a day-to-day basis?" If so, go along with the accepted practices and push aside your concerns about them, because you are likely to get fired if you wear your concerns on your sleeve. Or if you feel you can't abide these practices, then it's time to gracefully quit, hope for a good recommendation, and move on to something else that's more to your liking. As they say, you can't fit a square peg in a round hole. If your boss is like that round hole and you are that square peg, you aren't going to fit in unless you reshape your edges. If you can't do that, then look for that square hole where you will fit. Make your choice by becoming aware of and understanding the situation, realizing that you can't do much, if anything, to change it now. Then, do what feels most comfortable for you.

Today's Take-Aways

- ☑ If there isn't a good fit between you and the organizational culture you are in, find someplace where you will find a better fit.

- ☑ Think of yourself like a square peg: If your boss is a round hole, there's no point struggling to squeeze yourself in or complaining about round holes. Find a square hole that's right for you.

- ☑ If you feel uncomfortable playing with fire and can't turn down the heat, find someplace that's cool to play.

- ☑ Sometimes it's not the bad boss but the "bad industry" that's the problem. In that case, decide whether you can still have a good work experience there; if not, it's not a good place for you to stay and it's time to move on.

31

The Cover-Up

Sometimes a single uncomfortable incident can turn a good boss into a bad one when trying to keep the incident quiet leaves everyone involved with a bad taste in his mouth. Ironically, the incident itself may be simply an embarrassment, but add in a cover-up and the problem lingers. Though it may not be apparent to the boss, resentments boil just under the surface.

That's what happened when Emily, a woman in her twenties who worked as a copywriter in the business department of a magazine. Her boss, Reginald, was the publisher of the magazine. Reginald was a nice, affable man in his forties who supervised a small staff of a half dozen employees. She found him easygoing to work with and felt comfortable with his light-handed managerial style. He would give her instructions on what to do, offer some suggestions for the approach, review her copy, and make any final suggestions for changes.

But disaster struck after Emily had been with the company for about two years. Reginald, Emily, and a few other employees in the department went on a business trip to pitch the magazine for additional advertising. The trip involved traveling from city to city in two cars. One evening, after the group left a dinner in a posh restaurant, Reginald was pulled over for a DUI because his car had been weaving slightly on the road. He spent the night in jail. The next morning, he called his attorney and was released on bail. He quietly paid the DUI fine, and underwent the usual DUI counseling and suspended license for several months to settle the case.

Yet for Emily, the incident had far deeper repercussions, even though she wasn't in Reginald's car when he was pulled over and arrested. Reginald asked everyone to say nothing about the incident, and no one did. Meanwhile, Emily found her relationship with Reginald deteriorating, though on the surface everything appeared normal as usual. She now felt uncomfortable and strained around him, and she became disillusioned with Reginald when he and others in middle management asked her and other employees to keep the incident to themselves. The request erased the previous image she had of the friendly, helpful, affable boss because now she felt the relationship was "inauthentic" and built on a lie.

Nothing was ever the same again. Though Emily continued to work for the company for another year after the incident and never mentioned it just as she was asked to do, the relationship wasn't "normal" because it felt phony. It was based on a cover-up. She just didn't trust or respect Reginald as before, and while she followed his professional advice and guidelines, she continually questioned his guidance in her mind. The cover-up had created issues of trust that stayed with her until she left the job about a year later to go into the editorial side of magazine publishing.

What Should Emily Have Done?

While Emily chose to remain in the job despite how uncomfortable it made her feel, she might have taken some steps to better deal with the situation. In Emily's place, what would you do and why? What do you think the outcomes of these different options would be? Here are some possibilities:

- ➲ Try to be a little more understanding, and let go of your feelings of resentment and disrespect towards Reginald since this was a one-time incident after a party on a business trip.

- ➲ Meet with Reginald in his office and have a heart-to-heart conversation with him during which you tell him how both the incident and the cover-up have bothered you.

⊃ Privately tell other staffers you like and trust about the incident and how you felt disturbed by the request to cover it up. The responses you get can help to validate your feelings and opinions, and perhaps soften them. Opening up may help you release any feelings of hurt and anger.

⊃ Bring up the incident at an office meeting, explaining that there shouldn't be such secrets in the office because they are interfering with your ability to do good work.

⊃ Leave an anonymous note about the incident on a desk for all to see so everyone in the office will know what happened and you don't have to say anything.

⊃ Keep working away quietly as you have been doing because it's better to go along to get along and get a good reference when you leave.

It would seem that the cover-up here is worse than the actual incident, which may have been embarrassing but little more. Sometimes even the best people can make a mistake in judgment after a convivial party. And perhaps others in the group share some responsibility for letting Reginald drive if he seemed to have had too much to drink after a party. In any event, apart from the cover-up, the incident resulted in limited harm, since it involved no accident or near accident. And Reginald did pay a hefty penalty for his transgression in the form of a fine and a night in jail.

Thus, perhaps Emily should have been less harsh in her judgment of Reginald following the incident since he had been a "good" boss in her eyes up to that point. Since it was the cover-up more than the incident itself that really bothered her, she might have done better to find a way encourage Reginald to come clean rather than breaching his request for confidentiality. For example, in Emily's situation you might ask to have a meeting with your boss to discuss an area of concern. Then, you could have a heart-to-heart talk with him. You could express how covering up what happened made you feel uncomfortable, and ask if he might consider letting others know what happened. You might point out that this incident could be used as a cautionary tale to others in the office about the perils of drinking and driving. You could even mention that people might find some humor in his having spent the night in jail.

Alternatively, if you decide not to bring up the incident with your boss, you might continue to work in your job as Emily did for a year. However, you would be wise to work on releasing your feelings of resentment for your own peace of mind. For example, Emily might remind herself how she had found Reginald a good boss to work with for two years before the incident and not let a single mishap destroy this positive relationship. Moreover, to help let go of her anger, Emily might remember that this incident didn't involve any threat or abuse against her and that it was an isolated mistake, not part of an ongoing drug or alcohol problem.

The best alternatives in this situation seem to be talking with the boss to get everything out on the table or choose to let it go. In other words, confront the issue in a straightforward manner to end any cover-up, or let it go because it isn't that important. Either of these approaches seems far superior to efforts to bringing the cover-up out in the open unilaterally by secretly talking about it, creating another embarrassing situation to reveal the incident publicly, or anonymously letting others know about it. In the first case, you are betraying a trust and promise of confidence with some behind-the-back maneuvering, while the other scenarios involve escalating the issue and running the risk of having it backfire, thus making you look bad and possibly costing you your job. As they say, it's good to forgive and forget, or in the immortal words of Don Quixote: "Let us forget and forgive injuries."

Today's Take-Aways

☑ Don't let your anger about the cover-up lead you to magnify your anger about the actual incident.

☑ If going along with a cover-up is what bothers you, think of ways to get whoever is pressuring you to keep quiet to fess up.

☑ If you can't forget, try to forgive; you'll feel better, especially if you plan to keep working together.

☑ Sometimes bad bosses aren't that bad; they are just human, not perfect.

It's a Crime!

Occasionally, bad bosses are so bad that they are actually committing crimes, and you know or suspect it, though others in the office might not. They are embezzling from the company, writing bad checks, hiring individuals or organizations for various services with no intention or money to pay, or committing any number of other misdeeds. Sometimes such behavior starts when a few exaggerations and lies get out of hand. Sometimes the problem is the boss is trying to save a struggling business by "borrowing" money he doesn't have. He thinks that once the business turns the corner, he can put the money back. And sometimes the boss thinks his great idea will eventually work—he just needs a little more money right now.

Whatever the reason, if the boss is committing a crime and you know or suspect it, you run the risk of being implicated yourself. You could even be accused of being an accomplice or accessory to the crime. An example might be if you follow your boss's instructions and your actions contribute to the commission of a crime, or if you happened to see your boss do something and said nothing, even though you should have known the action was not legal.

That's what happened to Michael, a former marketing manager, when he signed on for what he thought was a dream job as a tour escort. He looked on the job as a relaxing break from the heavy pressure of his last few marketing jobs. At first, he felt fortunate. His job involved going on romantic singles cruises where there were more single women than men. His salary was small, but the perk of the free cruises made up for it. His assignment, according to his new boss, Rex, was to "just chat up and dance with the women, but no sex." What could be easier?

Rex was very impressive and had charm and charisma to spare. He said he had moved to California to set up a branch of a big East Coast travel agency where he was a vice president. Rex had photos of the company's planes and described how he used them to jet around the country looking for new franchise locations for the company. Now he was in California to run the company, and he planned to focus on creating travel programs for singles.

Soon, Rex had a dozen or so escorts on tap for the tours, a new vice president of travel sales, and a blonde, twentysomething secretary who looked like a model. He set up a trendy-looking corporate office suite with a half dozen rooms, including a board room with a long table for meetings. Rex began having meetings every week to plan different programs, and he invited all of the tour escorts to attend these meetings to contribute their suggestions. Plus, he wanted to create a warm, family feeling for everyone in the company.

After several weeks, however, Michael began to feel the meetings were mostly devoted to dreamy discussions about the great trips that the company hoped to set up, and he observed that Rex didn't seem to know what to do to start promoting the trips in the local media or through creating tie-ins with local singles organizations. So Michael began to offer suggestions, thinking Rex was just unfamiliar with the media and the world of singles groups in northern California. Soon, Rex invited him to become the tour group's marketing manager, which meant helping to create travel brochures, put on a few welcoming parties for the local business community, and buy ads in local singles magazines. Michael agreed and continued to attend the meetings, listen to the conversations about glorious singles trips, and help put on parties. Supposedly, these parties were a way to reach out to the young, professional singles who were part of the business community and would want to go on these trips. But many people came just because these were great parties with great hors d'oeuvres and a chance to mix and mingle with other professionals in a trendy atmosphere.

After a few more weeks, Michael noticed that none of the customers had actually gone on one of the trips. Only a few couples had booked a tropical cruise for the Christmas holidays, and that was still several months away. The staff, worried that business wasn't going too well, suggested to Rex that perhaps the word "singles" was a turn-off, something associated with pick-up bars. Rex wasn't interested in their recommendations, however, and he forged ahead with his original plan. That's when Michael began to notice assorted warning signs that something was amiss.

Repeatedly, Rex used his charm to persuade vendors to give him credit, promising to pay as soon as expected funds from headquarters came through. Meanwhile, Michael kept churning out tantalizing flyers for glamorous trips to exotic locations. But there were never enough people signing up for any of the trips to actually take place, though Rex kept taking in deposits and telling clients they would be on the next trip.

Meanwhile, there were increasing signs of money problems. Rex moved the company account from bank to bank, claiming that each one didn't understand how to work with his kind of business. Then Rex had trouble making the payroll. When one of Michael's paychecks bounced, Rex calmly assured him the problem was some confusion at the bank. He acted like nothing was wrong, relying on his usual debonair charm that was so persuasive with everyone. So Michael remained on board. He didn't want to recognize that the boss who charmed everyone was not sincere. And Michael did get paid, though it took several weeks for his check to clear.

What Should Michael Do Now, if Anything?

So was the check bouncing incident just a temporary hiccup for a new business, or was it a warning of serious dangers ahead? In Michael's place, what would you have done and why? What do you think the outcomes of these different options would be? Here are some possibilities:

➲ Set up a meeting to talk with Rex to point out why his plan for singles trips wasn't working and would lead to financial problems. Quit if he doesn't change his approach.

➲ If Rex misses another payment or bounces another check, stop working and advise him you will only return to work for him once you are paid.

- ⊃ Set up individual meetings with other tour escorts and staffers to explain your concerns and alert others.

- ⊃ Contact the clients you think have been duped and urge them to get their money back.

- ⊃ File a small claims suit to recover your bounced paycheck and be ready to serve Rex at the big singles gala if the party isn't successful, since if that occurs, it will be clear that Rex won't succeed.

- ⊃ Contact the local police or your district attorney's fraud unit to explain your concerns and be willing to cooperate. This way, at least you've covered yourself from any liability for the fraud.

This is the kind of situation where it's best to act sooner rather than wait until the inevitable crash. It can be tempting to stay aboard, hoping that things will turn around, particularly when your boss seems so charming and others are drawn by his charisma. A boss like Rex can create a really fun working atmosphere. But it's important not to let the perceptions and beliefs of others undermine your own more perceptive insights.

In this case, as soon as Michael began to see the warning signs, he should have investigated what was going on more closely. Once he realized that Rex's plan wasn't going to work, he should have taken immediate action. A good way to start would be to meet with Rex and have a serious discussion about his concerns. If Rex didn't listen, that would have been a good time to get out or prepare an exit strategy.

Also, in light of the other warning signs, Michael should have refused to do further work or cut back to doing only a limited amount of work the first time Rex missed a paycheck. Perhaps he could have explained it by saying he needed to take on other work in the meantime. This would be a way to monitor the situation and clarify if the problem was just due to Rex's going through a difficult start-up period or if something more sinister was going on. With this approach, you might be able to make a quicker getaway and lose less time and money than Michael actually did.

What really happened here is that Michael nursed his growing doubts while trying to give Rex the benefit of the doubt, and meanwhile, the promotional parties continued with local business executives and young singles, and Rex playing the genial host. It was a role Rex was a great success at playing, and he really preferred the aura of local celebrity to the more serious day-to-day responsibilities of running a business. Meanwhile, people continued to be captivated by Rex. Even when Michael shared his concerns with a few other tour escorts as the weeks slipped by, no one else seemed to want to acknowledge there could be a problem and risk upsetting the fun rounds of parties and aura of glamour that Rex exuded.

So for a few weeks, Michael hesitated and wondered what to do. The ax finally fell at a gala singles event organized by Rex. He had hoped for at least 300 attendees who would pay $35 each to attend the event. The idea was that the cover charges would pay for the cost of the party and then enough people would sign up for trips so he could cover other expenses and debts for the past three months. Unfortunately, the event was poorly attended. In the end, only 100 singles showed up, and about half of these were comped admissions, meaning they were free. The next day Rex fled his small apartment, leaving in his wake several bounced checks to the hotel, musicians, and caterer, all of whom he had charmed into accepting a check for payment in full the night of the party, rather than getting a deposit as was the norm.

Michael and the other staffers didn't have the slightest idea where Rex had gone, though they soon heard from the vendors with the bounced checks. A few days later, they heard from the police, too. Rex had been stopped in southern California when he made an illegal left turn. When the police did a warrants check, they discovered he was wanted up north. There was a stolen credit card machine in his car; presumably Rex planned to finance a new start in southern California that way. He was charged with grand theft for more than $14,000 in bounced checks that final night, though there was about $50,000 in other payments from clients that were also outstanding.

Fortunately, the police treated Michael and the other staffers like innocent dupes who had been suckered in by Rex's charm. Yet Michael felt that they might have easily accused him, too, since he had continued to work for and help Rex despite his mounting suspicions that something was wrong. He felt lucky to get away with only a few thousand dollars in unpaid earnings, but regretted that he hadn't done something sooner to stop the looming disaster.

In this case, it seems like Michael was in a murky situation where it wasn't clear whether he was observing the birth pangs of a new business or a growing train wreck that would lead to criminal activity. In such a situation where you have suspicions but aren't certain, you must proceed very cautiously.

For example, the decision about whether to share concerns with other staffers has to be made on an individual basis. On one hand, you have to be careful about making public accusations before you have sufficient evidence to reasonably support the accusation. In this case, without clear proof of what Rex was doing, an accusation could amount to defamation, which is damage to a person's reputation by making a false statement about them.

Deciding whether or not to go to the police is also an important consideration. Though initially Rex's actions might not constitute a crime, if you have your suspicions, it is a good idea to at least make a report to the police. You can do this in confidence if you like, since you don't want to press any charges. By reporting your concerns, however, you have at least alerted the police to a possible crime and have protected yourself if your suspicions prove to be well founded. The police can also advise you about what to do when you aren't sure, so you can avoid engaging in criminal behavior yourself. Initially, the police might be unlikely to act on just the strength of your lone suspicions, since this probably would not rise to the level of "probable cause." But they would have your report on record and could rely on it were they to get complaints from others that might indicate a pattern of criminal behavior. That would give them enough to go on to take some action, such as contacting Rex and letting him know—without mentioning any names—that he has been the subject of a number of complaints. Then they could ask further questions to learn what is going on. In fact, if they got these complaints soon enough they might have been able to head off Rex at the pass, before he had to flee town after the disastrous singles gala.

In short, take seriously the warning signs that things are wrong. Pay attention and observe to see if these warnings are confirmed. Try to take steps early on to see if you can do something to correct the course, especially if you feel your boss is being drawn into criminal activity due to circumstances and not that she set out to engage in fraud. In the latter case, where you suspect the illegal activity may be intentional, you should immediately act to get out and contact the police or district attorney's fraud unit. Then, if your boss isn't amenable to making changes, it's best to leave as quickly as possible and get as much as is due to you as possible. Don't let a boss's charm and charisma blind you to the cold, hard facts of what is really going on.

Today's Take-Aways

- ☑ If you think your boss is committing crimes, it can be a crime to keep working there or to fail to report what you suspect to the authorities.

- ☑ If your boss is a great con artist with lots of charisma, you may be the first to know before anyone else suspects anything. Don't be the last to get out.

- ☑ If you think your boss could end up with a record, start keeping records and telling authorities for the record, so you don't wind up with a record of your own.

33

Sex and Faxes

As people today spend more of their time in the workplace, office romances are blossoming. But they can be disruptive, and when they involve a boss and an employee, they can be grounds for sexual harassment if the subordinate later complains. They could provide the grounds for a "hostile workplace environment" if other employees were to find out and complain. These are both reasons that these boss-employee relationships are now prohibited in most company policy manuals. Not only can the romance lead to problems for the employee should things go bad and lead to a messy breakup, but others in the office can experience feelings of jealousy, complain about favoritism, and feel their own promotional opportunities jeopardized by a boss who decides from the heart rather than on performance. So what should you do as an employee who is out of the romantic loop but feels that workplace relationships are being compromised by a boss's libido?

That's what happened for Erin, when she worked as an administrative assistant to Harrison, one of several account executives in a small ad agency. She loved the job, her first after graduating with a business degree. At first, she felt she had a wonderfully charming boss who was helpful in teaching her the ropes. She also felt he was usually good at communicating assignments and giving her guidelines about how to prioritize the work. Occasionally, though, he seemed distracted and failed to give her the deadlines until they were almost on top of her. She had to work overtime or on weekends to catch up, but she didn't mind too much because she got time and a half for those hours.

Then, one Friday, it happened: Erin had some papers to leave on Harrison's desk. The office door was closed, so she knocked. After hearing no response, she opened the door only to find Harrison and one of the other assistants, Betty, wrapped in each other's arms on the floor. She quickly excused herself in embarrassment, and soon afterward, Harrison came over to her desk and told her to never come into his office again without knocking. He made no apologies.

After that incident, Erin felt very uncomfortable in the office. While she made sure not to enter Harrison's office without knocking, she also worried that he might find a way of firing her because she knew of his affair with Betty. She worried, too, that Betty might get a promotion or extra perks because of her affair, and that even if Harrison didn't fire her, she might be at a disadvantage when it came to moving ahead.

Outwardly, Harrison acted like nothing had happened, but Erin wasn't sure she could trust him. She now noticed when Betty went off to see Harrison in his office, ostensibly to get a new assignment. Each time, she wondered if they might be getting together for some on-site lovemaking. Later, when she learned Harrison was married, she was even more perturbed by the fact that he was cheating on his wife.

Erin was at a loss for what to do: She didn't want to leave the company because she felt her job was an ideal stepping stone toward a career as an account executive. But she worried what would happen if she continued working for Harrison.

What Should Erin Do?

In Erin's place, what would you do and why? What do you think the outcomes of these different options would be? Here are some possibilities:

➲ Continue to look the other way and play nice with Harrison so he feels he has nothing to fear from your discovery.

⮑ Arrange for a private meeting with Harrison and tell him you don't think his behavior is appropriate and could undermine the morale and productivity of others in the office.

⮑ Send an anonymous memo to Harrison's boss to let him know that Harrison is fooling around with someone in the office.

⮑ Meet with human resources and complain about what Harrison is doing.

⮑ Speak to one or more other coworkers besides Betty to determine if they are aware of what's going on and learn what they might want to do as a group to deal with the situation

⮑ Recruit one or two trusted coworkers to join you when you think that Harrison and Betty are having a lovemaking session in his office. When you all walk in on them, Harrison will know that you aren't the only one in the office who knows what he's he doing, and he will have to deal openly with the situation.

⮑ Make an anonymous phone call to Harrison's wife to let her know that he is having an affair with someone in the workplace and hope that she will bust up the relationship.

This is definitely a tricky situation. Your boss is out of line, but as a relatively new employee, you have little clout. It's probably best to avoid trying to do anything anonymously, since such memos and phone calls have a way of surfacing and could backfire on you. Also, if you are the only one who knows about the tryst, it might be easy for Harrison and Betty to deny anything happened. If you try to raise the issue on your own, you could well be out the door sooner rather than later because your boss might be able to find reasons why your work is not acceptable. And a wrongful termination lawsuit is probably not the best way to build a track record to move on in this career.

One approach might be to play it close to the vest for awhile, and perhaps start keeping a private notebook where you date and record your observations about the affair. But keep it somewhere out of the office so it stays private. Meanwhile, look for allies among other coworkers with whom you can share what happened. Or perhaps find an auspicious occasion when they can observe for themselves what is going on in Harrison's office if they don't already know. This way, you can build up your power base in the organization by letting others know what is going on and they can feel equally disturbed. Together, you can come up with different scenarios for bringing this fling out in the open, such as arranging for a meeting at your boss's office as a group to tell him you feel the affair is interfering with work in the office. Or if this is a large enough office with human resources department, go as a group to HR to complain since Harrison's actions could be the basis for creating a hostile working environment.

Or perhaps you can find a time when the group can "unexpectedly" walk in on your boss in an amorous tryst. This approach would likely put a stop to the behavior. Once his secret is out and spreading around the office, he's going to be thinking about damage control, not getting back at you. If you can arrange such a surprise outing of the affair, you will also have the relief of being only one of a group in the office involved in this situation. You avoid the repercussions of being the only one who knows, and the lone whistleblower risking repercussions.

Today's Take-Aways

- ☑ It can be dangerous to be the only one who knows a secret, so do what you can to quietly spread the word.

- ☑ If you have little power, you can quickly be shut down if you try to blow the whistle. Find others to blow the whistle with you.

When a boss opens the door to love with an employee, find ways to open the door wide enough so others beside you know what's going on.

34

Give In to Collective Denial or Leave?

Sometimes, even when you're right that a bad boss is undermining office morale and productivity, you may still have to face the political reality that no one wants to acknowledge how bad things are. So you may have to make a choice: Do you simply shut up and take the go-along-to-get-along approach? Or do you leave? Sometimes leaving may be the best alternative rather than joining in a collective denial. However, some specific incident eventually may break through the denial, and your former bad boss may be out the door. In fact, your leaving could even be the trigger that leads to this outcome, which might be a satisfying "I told you so" result when you hear about it, even if you are no longer there.

That's what happened to Karen when she joined a staff of counselors who helped to counsel women on domestic violence issues. She and several other counselors were assigned to work for a coordinator named Andrea, while a half dozen other counselors worked under two other coordinators. On top of the organization was an executive director. Soon after Karen came aboard, she began to see that Andrea had problems. Andrea was a frequently surly, critical person who was continually telling her staff members what they did wrong, such as the way they wrote up case notes or talked to clients on the phone. Sometimes she would even accuse them of making a mistake when they had carefully followed her directions. In response, Karen found that the other counselors usually apologized and backed down. To keep office relationships working smoothly, they would simply say "yes" to whatever Andrea said, even when she was wrong.

"Andrea picked up on the little details of those working under her," Karen said. She consistently downgraded their skills, to the point of reducing some people to tears, after which she would become very sweet for awhile, saying 'You don't have to cry; you'll make mistakes.' But then she would turn threatening, saying: 'Just don't do it again.' And once the person made another mistake, the process would begin again." Another problem was that Andrea would often change the rules and then put people down when they inevitably made a mistake because of the new, poorly explained policy. The usual response of the staffers, according to Karen, was to "try to anticipate what Andrea wanted in order to please her, or to apologize, saying 'I'm so sorry,' 'I must have misunderstood,' or 'I'll fix it.'"

But were Karen's perceptions accurate? One day, after being on the job for about two weeks, Karen decided to check them out. While on the elevator with several other counselors, some of whom worked directly for Andrea, she briefly described what she thought was "an abusive dynamic coming from the coordinator." When the elevator came to the first floor, there was total silence as everyone got out, but one woman stayed behind, telling Karen, "You hit the nail on the head, but none of us want to be accused of facing off against her." Then the woman invited Karen to "call me if you want to talk more about this."

When Karen did call her, the woman explained how many other counselors had left the organization as a result of Andrea's abusive nature. Andrea was too mean to them, and they didn't want to confront her. So they accepted the put-downs and walking on the eggshells that came with the territory until they were able to get out from under her thumb. By contrast, Karen decided to stand up for herself and challenge Andrea when she disagreed with Andrea's directives. At once it was like a *High Noon*-style showdown, with Andrea out to catch Karen in the smallest mistakes. In response, Karen began to keep notes of Andrea's criticisms so she could compare what her boss said then and now. When Andrea told her something else later on, Karen could tell her: "But this is what you told me before," and whip out her notes to show this.

While Karen may have been right, the tactic made Andrea angry. "Instead of using my skills as a facilitator and problem solver, I became a threat," Karen explained. "So Andrea began to ride my back, looking at everything I wrote, listening in when I was on the phone, checking up on wherever I went. She also went to the executive director and told negative stories about how I wasn't getting along with others on the staff. But when the executive director checked with the other staff members, she heard different stories from them, including complaints about the coordinator."

Although Karen's willingness to stand up to the coordinator helped to shed light on what was going on, leading to Andrea's eventual departure from the organization, at the time, no one wanted to acknowledge the problem. It was a kind of head-in-the-sand, ostrich approach; people continued to work, but didn't dare to talk about the real problem.

At the end of her second month there, Karen began to organize a retreat at which staff members would come together as a support group to talk about the problems they faced and how to resolve them. Planning the retreat turned out to be the beginning of the end. "Once I started to design the retreat, I was a real threat, and Andrea became very paranoid and went to the executive director," Karen said. "She complained that I was not a good person to organize the retreat since I was causing morale problems and spreading bad stories about her, and she told me to stop organizing the retreat. When I said I was just trying to help deal with the increasing tension in the office, she said, 'I don't know what you are talking about. There is no problem. Just you.'"

In response, Karen typed up her notes of every incident, went to the executive director, and asked to meet with her personally to present these documents and discuss the problems with her. Instead of meeting with her individually, however, the executive director insisted that Andrea be there, too, so Karen had to present her case against Andrea in front of Andrea. Karen prefaced the meeting by saying she wanted to describe what happened so "we can gain insights about what we might do to change this," but the discussion quickly turned into a confrontation. As Karen presented her material, Andrea glared at her like the enemy. After Karen finished, the executive director looked at her sternly and said, "You have two choices: You can stay on the job you have with no changes, or you can leave the organization."

Karen resigned, though her challenge to the coordinator helped to lead to the changes she felt were needed. The new staff member hired by the executive director to replace Karen left after only three weeks. Soon after that, Andrea asked to go on medical leave, and within a few weeks, Andrea was permanently out of the organization, too. Meanwhile, feeling glad she had stood her ground, Karen found another counseling job in a much more agreeable organization. Her only regret was that "they didn't make these changes on my watch. I could have caved and been like the others, found a way to work around her, or apologized for my various mistakes which I didn't think I made. But I felt I had to leave because otherwise, working in that environment was like being stuck in a bad marriage. No one wanted to acknowledge that anything was seriously wrong until after I left."

What Should Karen Have Done?

Was leaving the best choice? Is there anything Karen might have done differently or did she make the best choice at the time? In Karen's place, what would you do and why? What do you think the outcomes of these different options would be? Here are some possibilities:

⮑   Follow the same strategy as everyone else: Either say yes or avoid the boss since that's the best way to get along.

⮑   Stand up to Andrea yourself, but don't try to organize others in the office to share problems as a group, such as at a retreat, since attitudes are entrenched and you are new to the organization.

⮑   Put in for a transfer to another department early on without complaining about your boss's poor management style. Find some other plausible reason so you can leave more gracefully.

⮑   Set up a private meeting with Andrea to go over the series of problems you have encountered. Explain how you really would like to work things out so you can perform as she wants, but tell her that you hope you can also share your ideas.

➲ Stand up to Andrea, try to organize a retreat, and talk to the
    executive director, as Karen did. It's better to bring things out in
    the open with everyone. If they aren't ready to deal with the
    problems, it's better to leave.

In this case, Karen came into an organization with a culture of denial, a boss who didn't want anyone to challenge her decisions, even
when she was wrong, and a group of coworkers who agreeably went
along with her to keep the peace. One irony is that this was an organization of women helping the victims of domestic violence stand
up for themselves to stop the abuse or leave an abusive situation.
Yet, at the same time, they were going along with an abusive controlling boss themselves—a situation Karen recognized within two
weeks on the job. She essentially had two choices: Step into a co-
dependent role to support the boss like the other employees, or work
for change, which would mean enabling the staff members to take
on more power for themselves.

     In some cases, going along with things as they are might be a
good choice, such as if you've recently landed a job in a tight market
or the move is the beginning of a new career. But as you gain more
experience, it may be worth taking a stand, and doing so might even
help you gain insights to apply in better understanding the dynamics
in other organizational settings.

     Karen was willing to risk choosing the second option of working
to raise awareness of the problem in order to help resolve it, so she
took a good first step by documenting exactly what the problem was.
For example, she noted what instructions were given originally,
since Andrea was prone to give subsequent instructions and then
blame the staffers for doing the wrong thing. However, you might
get better results in seeking change by approaching your boss in a
less confrontational way, such as by setting up a one-on-one meeting
to go over the problems you have documented. At this meeting, you
might set the stage for reconciliation by being more gentle or diplomatic in your approach, emphasizing how you want to help and explaining that you are not trying to undermine your boss's role. If
Karen had done this, Andrea might not have felt so threatened by
her taking a stand and might have been more willing to bend.

     Once it became clear that Andrea was trying to undermine Karen
by spreading false, negative stories, approaching the executive direc-

tor was a good next step, although the executive director should have been willing to listen to Karen's complaint before bringing Andrea into the discussion. Since that didn't happen, Karen was able to rely on the documentation she had written to support her cause, and that helped to show she was right about the abusive climate Andrea created. However, since the director continued to support the head-in-the-sand attitude of the whole organization, Karen was still faced with the same two choices: Remain silent like the others or leave.

Under the circumstances, having made the initial choice to stand up, it made the most sense to continue to take a stand by leaving—a risk that paid off in Karen's case with a better job in a more open, supportive environment. And ultimately, her perception of the problems in the organization was supported by the quick departure of her replacement and by the fact that Andrea had been exposed by Karen's efforts to bring the abusive climate she created out in the open.

Once you have stood up to your boss and have been stonewalled by her boss, can you turn around and make the other choice to go along? Probably not. That would be like retreating into silence with a boss who already views you as a threat, and she might easily retaliate. As Karen's story illustrates, there are times when you may feel it necessary to take a stand. But once you do, be ready to move on if that stand doesn't bring about the desired change. If the boss is creating an abusive climate and the organization is in denial supporting that atmosphere and not ready to change, it might be best to work for change rather than going along. But if the organization isn't ready for that change, it may be time to make the change for yourself.

Today's Take-Aways

- ☑ If you can't change an organization in denial over a climate of abuse, consider changing the organization you are in.

- ☑ Do you have the choice: Stand up for change or give in. Once you are aware of your options and outcomes, you can make the best choice for you.

- ☑ Often when a boss is manipulative and abusive, you'll find a code of silence and submission that helps everyone get along. Should you go along with that code or stand up against it? The choice is up to you.

Part VI

Putting It All Together

Bad Boss or Bad Employee?

Sometimes you think you've got a bad boss when the real problem is that you are a bad employee, but don't know it. This may be particularly true if you have a series of complaints about bad bosses, and the conflicts show a pattern—or the bosses make similar complaints about you. In that case, rather than thinking about how to deal with a bad boss, consider how you might change yourself.

Often it can be hard to recognize this situation because, as research by psychologists has shown, people don't like to blame themselves for problems. We generally like to take the credit when something goes well; we tend to think the outcome is due to our abilities and actions. By contrast, when things go wrong, we seek to put the responsibility outside of ourselves and onto others, or to bad luck in general, so we don't have to take the blame. But if you want to overcome a problem that can seriously hamper your career progress, you have to make an effort to overcome this natural tendency to blame others rather than yourself.

If you see a continuing pattern of bad boss problems, take some time to reflect on whether the problem might be you. Even when you first think you have a bad boss, particularly if you are the only one with this complaint, take a close look at yourself. Otherwise, you might be unlikely to recognize that you are the main source of the problem.

That's what happened to Judy, who reported a series of problems with bad bosses, in a number of different fields. In the first case, she was hired as an operations and production assistant for a small magazine through the HR department. She had majored in communications at college and had interned on the school paper for over a year. Her job was to help in laying out the paper on the computer, as well as to purchase supplies, run copies, and keep track of and file advertising orders. But soon Judy found herself locked in a conflict with her supervisor, Paul. She complained he was insulting when he told her that he didn't understand how she had been hired because she seemed so disorganized and slow, and repeatedly didn't follow instructions. He even called her "stupid" once when she put some files in the wrong place, and complained that it cost the company more to have her work for them than if they hired two people to do her job or paid someone else twice as much. He said "no one liked her," and the only reason he kept her in the job was because it was so difficult to fire anyone due to company policies. Though Judy tried various strategies, from talking to Paul about her work to trying to speed up doing the tasks, nothing seemed to be good enough for him, and this left her feeling dispirited and frustrated.

Judy considered bringing in a lawyer to fight for her, but finally decided to move on. Her next job was as an office assistant providing support for the sales reps at a large financial services company. Her job was to answer phones, record the sales made by each rep, and keep up the database. When she was hired, her boss, Alice, told her that she could expect a promotion and raise after about three months. But after a few months, though Judy thought she was doing a good job, Alice told her, "You're not good on the phones and you're too slow entering the data into the computer." Judy tried to do better, but at the next review, Alice told her much the same thing: She was still too slow and needed to improve on the phone. Soon after that, Judy noticed that other assistants hired after her were promoted and given raises while Alice had passed her by. Judy sensed that Alice might be getting ready to fire her and filed a complaint with human resources, but ultimately she decided she would rather start over in another job. So she quit.

A series of jobs followed, all of which lasted about four to six months each, and in every one, Judy always had a problem with the boss. In one job, she was hired to coordinate the drivers for an airport van service, and she complained her boss was unfair because she had to work a longer and more difficult shift than other employees. She claimed that was why she mixed up the orders to drivers more than the other coordinators. Additionally, Judy complained that her boss insulted her when he criticized her screw-ups, telling her that she was stupid for having made them and that she should be more careful in the future. But his insults made her so mad that, after trying to be careful about the orders, she quit this job, too.

In another case, where she was hired as a marketing assistant to do cold calling and follow up to close sales for a lighting company, she felt angry because her boss had promised to give her a promotion and raise her commission rate after she was there for three months, but neither had materialized. Why? Because, he said, she wasn't closing enough sales and wasn't keeping good enough records to track her sales. In frustration, Judy quit that job, too—and the next, and the next, all for similar reasons.

When I met her at a business networking event, Judy had plenty of bad boss stories to share. Though the settings were all different, it was obvious after hearing a few of them that they echoed a pattern. Perhaps each of her bosses did have some difficulty in communicating what they wanted; maybe they should have provided her with more training, and ideally, they could have been more diplomatic and less abrasive in telling Judy what she did wrong. But beyond that, there seemed to be an overall pattern: Judy was going from job to job, and having similar problems at all of the companies. Yet, in each case, Judy blamed the bosses, claiming they were insulting, unfair, made promises they didn't keep, and so on. She didn't have a clue that she might be doing something wrong herself, which is often the case when there is a pattern of problems on different jobs. Judy claimed she just had a run of bad luck and ended up with a bunch of bad bosses, which seemed unlikely on such a continuing basis.

What Should Judy Have Done Differently and What Should She Do Now?

Is there anything Judy might have done differently or that she could do now? In Judy's place, what would you do and why? What do you think the outcomes of these different options would be? Here are some possibilities:

- ➲ Instead of quitting, wait to be fired and pursue a wrongful termination claim on the grounds that you weren't properly trained.

- ➲ Set up meetings with your bosses after they complain about your performance so you can ask for more feedback and training in order to improve.

- ➲ Reconsider your choice of career. Maybe you aren't so good with detailed work and would enjoy another type of work, such as working outdoors or face-to-face with customers.

- ➲ Look more closely at why your bosses are saying you are too slow or make too many mistakes. Maybe you are distracted, bored, unmotivated, or have some other problem with doing the work.

- ➲ Be more patient in getting ahead, and focus on better learning how to do the job when you are first hired.

- ➲ Document whenever you feel your boss has insulted you or put you down, so you can use this written record in later filing a complaint or lawsuit.

In a case like this, given the pattern of repeated problems and bosses with similar complaints about the quality of your work, look more closely at yourself and at what your bosses have been telling you that you are doing wrong. Rather than focusing on your objections to the way your bosses have given you this information and feeling insulted and unfairly treated, you would do better to take a longer view as to how your own work may fall short so you can improve. If possible, ask your boss for more detailed and constructive feedback about what to do. Alternatively, think about how you might correct your work yourself, such as by paying more attention to what you are doing, reviewing what you are going to do while at home, practicing new tasks before you do them, or even making a game of routine work to make it more engaging and interesting so you can complete it more quickly and with fewer errors.

Documenting what is going on might be helpful, too. If the problem really does lie with your boss, you will have that information to use in making your case about unfair or improper treatment or wrongful termination. Alternatively, this documentation can help you identify when you are doing something wrong so you can work on improving. Consider whatever you write as though it is a work improvement diary. As you identify what you are doing wrong, also include your efforts to improve and chart your progress.

In short, don't just chalk up your work problems to having a bad boss, especially when the problems keep occurring in different settings and different types of jobs. The real problem may not be the bad boss—it might be you! If so, work on fixing yourself rather than trying to come up with ways to deal with a bad boss who isn't really that bad.

Today's Take-Aways

- ☑ If you have a pattern of problems on the job, consider the source of the problem. It may not be the bad boss—it may be you!

- ☑ It's easy to cast blame on someone else, but it's much harder to accept blame when the problem lies with you.

- ☑ It can be easier to accept blame for doing something wrong if you think of it as taking on responsibility.

- ☑ Is the problem you, your boss, or both? To fix the problem, you've got to understand it first.

36

How Bad Is Your Boss?
An Assessment Quiz

How bad is your boss, really? How difficult is the situation you have to cope with? This quiz will help you rate your situation compared to others so you can better put your own boss in perspective. After all, you may think your boss is really bad in some ways, but not so bad in others, while other people may have a boss who is bad in many ways. This quiz will help you better understand what to do to deal with your situation, from making the best of it, to having a conversation, to bringing in a neutral third party or advocate, to moving on—preferably with a good reference.

These 25 questions are based on the major issues raised in this book. Just rate how bad you think your boss is in each area. Answer as honestly as you can so you can most accurately assess your situation. Understanding is the first step to finding a solution.

Rate your boss on a scale from 0–4 on each question and then add up the totals. See the scoring key at the end to see how your boss rates. When there are two questions under a heading, these usually reflect extremes of behavior. So your boss is likely to rate bad for only one of these questions—unless of course, he engages in both types of bad behavior at different times (in which case, you're in even more trouble).

	RATING **(from 0–4)**

AGGRESSIVENESS

1. My boss is too aggressive in the way he gives orders and tells me what to do. _____
2. My boss is too weak and wishy-washy; he is too much of a pushover. _____

CONTROL

3. My boss is too domineering and controlling; he wants to micromanage everything. _____
4. My boss is overly disorganized and he often doesn't have a clue about what's going on; he delegates too much and loses control. _____

DECISIVENESS

5. My boss often makes snap or bad decisions or doesn't take into consideration what others want. _____
6. My boss is indecisive and has difficulty making any decisions so often things just happen. He keeps changing his mind, or I end up deciding for him. _____

COMMUNICATION

7. My boss is a poor communicator because he often yells and screams or speaks in rude and insulting ways. _____
8. My boss is a poor communicator because he doesn't explain or provide needed information very well. _____

GAMESMANSHIP

9. I feel like my boss is playing power games with me, such as by ordering me to do things just to get me to do them, all simply to show his power. _____
10. I feel like my boss is playing power games with others in the office and I am caught in this struggle between two bosses. _____

SEX IN THE OFFICE
11. I feel like my boss is taking advantage of his position by hitting on me. _____
12. I am disturbed that my boss is having a relationship with someone else in the office. _____

IT'S A CRIME
13. I believe my boss is involved in criminal activities and wants me to cover up for him. _____
14. My boss wants me to engage in some illegal or criminal activities and I don't feel comfortable doing so. _____

TRUST AND KEEPING PROMISES
15. I don't trust my boss because he makes promises to me and then doesn't follow through. _____
16. I don't trust my boss because he frequently lies to me and others. _____

FAIRNESS AND FLEXIBILITY
17. I don't think my boss is fair because he plays favorites in the office or doesn't give me the proper recognition for what I do. _____
18. I think my boss is too rigid and inflexible and doesn't adapt to the situation. _____

IN SEARCH OF PERFECTION
19. I think my boss is an unreasonable perfectionist, and he continually makes me do things unnecessarily to get it absolutely right. _____

A LACK OF TRAINING
20. My boss is terrible at providing training, instruction, and education, so I often am not sure what I am doing or am supposed to do. _____

NOT REALLY A MANAGER

21. While my boss has a lot of technical knowledge, he doesn't have any management skills, and mostly works on his own projects without trying to manage or lead others.

CONSIDERATION, COMPASSION, AND PERSONAL INTEREST

22. My boss shows a lack of sensitivity, consideration, or compassion for others, such as not being sympathetic when someone is sick or has family problems. _____

23. My boss is too much of a busybody because he wants to know too much about my personal life. _____

NO CREDIT

24. My boss unfairly takes the credit for other people's work and doesn't properly recognize people for the work they do. _____

EMOTIONAL AND UNPREDICTABLE

25. My boss is totally unpredictable because he is so emotional and blows hot and cold; I'm never sure what'll set him off. _____

TOTAL SCORE: _____

Rating System

Think of the results of this quiz as a flight report that can help you deal with the different types of captains you'll encounter during your flight through the sometimes friendly and sometimes not-so-friendly skies of the workplace. It's a guide to the overall difficulty of working with your boss. The lower the score, the better your boss is to work with; the higher the score, the more difficult he is to work with. Use the results to help assess how bad your boss really is and what you can do about it.

0–10 = Your boss is absolutely a dream boss to work for. Are you really sure he is that great?

10–19 = Generally, you've got a good boss, save just a few rough spots here and there.

20–29 = Your boss is starting to get difficult, but try to work through your problems before you throw in the towel.

30–39 = You've got serious pilot problems. Time to seriously deal with your problems or consider finding another boss.

40–59 = Mayday! Mayday! You could be in for a crash landing with a very difficult boss.

60–99 = Crack up! This is definitely a disaster. Get ready to crash and pull together the pieces after you land on your feet.

Knowing How to Deal

As the stories in the previous chapters have illustrated, it can be difficult to figure out what to do when dealing with a bad boss, and there are several possible alternatives in any given situation. You have to take many factors into consideration, and an optimal solution isn't always possible; rather, you have to pick the most reasonable alternative at the time. To help you decide, factor in your own personality, that of your boss, and how you interact together. The best solution for you may be different from what it might be for someone else with the same boss, or for someone facing a similar situation but in a different workplace.

For example, you may be willing to cope, hoping to better your chances for a promotion or good recommendation for another job elsewhere. But someone else may feel so enraged or frustrated that he has to confront the boss individually or with a group of workers to force changes, or leave the organization. And while some tyrannical bosses may act that way due to an excessive need for power, others may be holding the reins so tightly because they don't want to reveal their inner insecurities. In some cases, bad bosses may have the continuing support of higher-ups in the organization; in others, their own supervisors and top management may cease to back them up once they know of the problems. Or sometimes there's a pending merger or acquisition that may present the optimal time to air a pent-up grievance against the boss, since the new owners may be ready to get rid of a bad boss once they learn of the negative employee assessments, whereas previously, everyone was afraid to complain to higher management, or the top managers weren't prepared to listen or do anything.

Thus, you have to think through each situation differently. Once you have a greater understanding of the situation and your personal needs, wants, and priorities, then you can better decide what to do. The "What Should You Do?" questions in each chapter should get you started by giving you some possibilities to consider. While some are obviously wrong choices, likely to further inflame the conflict or otherwise fail, others could be real options. Thus, while I have provided suggestions on what to do, what someone should do or should have done will vary in any given situation or for different personalities. While one approach may be ideal for some people, that approach might not work as well for someone else.

Consider my suggestions to be like well-reasoned, common sense, creative, win-win possibilities for success in dealing with the boss, but keep in mind that other reasonable alternatives might still exist that could lead to success. In short, there's no exact science in figuring out the best approach to dealing with a bad boss, just as there's no exact way to promote good relationships, solve problems, or resolve workplace conflicts. Group relationships and the work environment with its mix of personalities, rules, regulations, customs, politics, and changing situations are too complex for simplistic, one-size-fits-all solutions. The same holds true for how you relate to your boss.

Still, it's possible that the methods presented in this book can help you better understand what is going on and prompt you to come up with a good choice or solution for dealing with the problem. You can then apply these different approaches, as appropriate, in dealing with your bad boss, or advising a friend or associate what they can do if they have a bad boss.

Accordingly, this last chapter is a discussion about bad bosses in general and what to do about them in different circumstances. Then, you can adapt this repertoire of methods to your particular situation, using different tools for strategizing and visualizing alternatives, and choosing the one you feel is right for you.

When Bosses Go Bad

It is easy to find reasons to criticize a boss for particular decisions or actions. It's also common to feel some resistance to following directions and orders from anyone in charge; they are directing you to do something, whether you want to do it or not. One person's definition of a bad boss may differ from another's, since you may find different personal qualities or actions objectionable. For example, you may really like a boss with a direct managing style because you like clear instructions about what to do, whereas someone who prefers working more independently may feel insulted and antagonized by too many orders. So a bad boss for one person may be a good boss for another. Managers or executives can avoid the bad boss label by adapting their managerial or leadership style to different employees with different needs and desires.

One way to determine what makes a bad boss is by thinking of all the things that bosses are supposed to do. A bad boss, then, would be someone who either doesn't do some of those things, or who takes that behavior to extremes, such as a boss who becomes a tyrant because he is too aggressive and controlling. At the other end of the spectrum is the boss who is too meek, indecisive, and disorganized, and fails to control or assert himself enough. Yet, while these are extremes, it helps to think of these qualities as existing along a continuum; a good or adequate boss goes bad if his behavior is too far in either direction. Also, a boss is bad if he doesn't engage in certain behaviors that he should, or engages in other behaviors that he shouldn't. An occasional slip into one of these behaviors may not be enough to make someone a bad boss, but if a boss continues to engage in those behaviors, he might qualify. Similarly, if a boss engages in multiple "bad boss" behaviors, that boss may qualify as bad even if none of these behaviors taken alone are that extreme.

The following list reflects common extremes of behavior that characterize a bad boss. You may come up with others, too.

1. Too aggressive . . . . .Not aggressive enough (weak and wishy-washy)
2. Too controlling and manipulative . . . . . Not controlling enough (includes playing power games)
3. Too organized and structured . . Unorganized and/or disorganized

4. Too rigid and inflexible . . . . .Too uncertain and vacillating

5. Too emotional . . . . Lacks compassion and empathy

6. Too much of a micromanager . . . . . . .Doesn't provide direction
or instruction
(or involved in own projects
and not interested in managing)

7. Makes impulsive or bad decisions . . . . .Indecisive

8. Too nosy and invasive . . . . . . Shows a lack of care and concern

Still other qualities identified as characterizing a bad boss include these:

9. Yells, screams, and is rude and insulting

10. Engages in sexual activity in the office by making unwanted sexual advances or being involved in a sexual relationship with an employee

11. Involved in criminal activities and asks employees to cover up or participate in these activities

12. Can't be trusted because he/she makes promises and doesn't keep them or lies

13. Unfair, in playing office favorites or not giving proper recognition or credit

14. Too much of a perfectionist

Some General Guidelines for What to Do

Every situation is different and needs to be strategized on a case-by-case basis, considering a number of key factors:

➲   Your boss's personality and reasons for the behavior

➲   Your organization's size, culture, norms, and standards

➲   Your own personality, needs, and career goals

➲   Your power and position compared to your boss

➲   Your boss's position in the organization or whether he is the owner

➲   How other employees feel about the boss's behavior

But before you consider specifics, here are some general guidelines to keep in mind when deciding how to respond. Weigh how these different factors might apply in your own situation.

➲ *Too aggressive, or too controlling and manipulative.* If your boss's behavior seems primarily due to a personality style, learn to adapt by staying out of the way when you can, or being friendly and accommodating to tame the beast. If the aggression stems from insecurity, take steps to reassure your boss that you are on top of things. For instance, you could send occasional memos with updates on what you are doing, ask your boss to clarify what he expects, or arrange a meeting to demonstrate that you understand what your boss expects you to do.

➲ *Not aggressive or controlling enough, or weak and wishy-washy.* Whether this behavior is a personality style or your boss's way of trying to empower employees, this is the time to take on more power for yourself. Since your boss has created a power vacuum, look for ways to fill it, and as you do, let your boss know you are doing this. In most cases, you will find that your boss appreciates your initiative. Also, look for opportunities to let others in the organization know what you are doing. Being proactive in this way could lead to a promotion, so get credit where you can. However, do it diplomatically, so you don't embarrass your boss or trigger jealousies for others in the company, which could backfire if you make your boss or others look bad to make yourself look good.

➲ *Too organized and structured, or too rigid and inflexible.* If this is more of a personality style, learn to adapt by becoming more organized and structured yourself. Say your boss is a stickler for time. Make it a point to be on time, even if you feel you can do better working on a more flexible time schedule. Your boss will feel more comfortable with you, and eventually may even ease up. Alternatively, if your boss is being rigid out of insecurity, try talking to him to show why things will work better if you make certain changes. Then, when things do work, document how and why they have been successful. After a while, your boss will feel more comfortable trying to do things in a way that is more efficient and productive, not to mention more satisfying to you.

⮑ *Too unorganized and/or disorganized, or too uncertain and vacillating.* In this case, whatever the reason for the behavior—a personality style or a boss who is too busy and frazzled to get organized—try to provide more organization yourself. Instead of feeling frustrated and fragmented with the disorder, take the initiative to create more order. It will not only make you feel better, but will also make the office more efficient and productive. Just be sure to let your boss know what you are doing. For example, don't just organize some messy piles of papers if you're the boss's assistant or secretary without first getting an approval. He may have a system for finding things in the disorder, and your organization will only get things lost. Explain your intentions first. Then, once your boss knows what you are doing and is agreeable, go ahead and create the more organized system. Or perhaps your boss is slow to make decisions. You might think through the decision you would like to see made and provide the supporting information to back up that decision. Your uncertain boss will probably be glad for your input and arrive at the decision you have presented. Or if your boss is forgetting to make an important decision, try discreetly reminding him that a decision needs to be made before the deadline.

⮑ *Too emotional.* If your boss is overly excitable, such as having a hair-trigger temper that makes you feel you are walking on eggshells when you are around him, a good approach is to become aware of what kind of things upset the boss. Then, stay out of the way when you see he is ready to explode about something. Or be ready to ride out the storm by remaining calm and detaching yourself from the situation. Perhaps you can seek to calm your boss with reassuring words, then move out of the way until he settles down.

⮑ *Lacks compassion and empathy.* In some cases, an uncaring boss may be something you just have to accept to keep the job, such as when the boss owns the company and wants employees to put work ahead of family. In other cases, you might try to negotiate an outcome that takes both your own and your boss's concerns into consideration and is acceptable to both of you. For instance, while your boss may not be moved by your family emergency, perhaps you can get him to agree to a beneficial exchange, such as by your offering to work several extra days next week in return for getting two days off to deal with a family emergency. Or perhaps you might be able to warm up your boss by finding something nice to do for him, such as giving a meaningful gift for a birthday or holiday.

➲ *Too much of a micromanager.* Generally, the boss who wants to know everything is driven by the same concerns as the overly controlling boss. He isn't sure you are going to do the job right, so find ways to reassure him that you will, such as by sending memos of your progress.

➲ *Too much of a perfectionist.* The same kind of strategy can work with the perfectionist boss as with the micromanager or over-controlling boss. Try reassuring him that you are on top of things and pay very close attention to detail, such as by proofing a letter extra carefully before you show it to your boss, so there are no mistakes. If this strategy doesn't work, try the art of detachment so you are more relaxed when your boss engages in unnecessary nitpicking.

➲ *Doesn't provide direction or instruction, or is involved in his own projects and not interested in managing.* If the problem is not having enough direction or instruction, ask for additional clarification, rather than feeling uncertain and confused and plunging ahead anyway and maybe getting it wrong. Set up a meeting in your boss's office individually, or as a group if others aren't sure what to do either. Or if your boss responds better to written communication, send your boss a memo or e-mail listing what you don't know. If your boss still won't tell you what you need to know, try going above your boss to someone else who can give you the direction you need. If the lack of direction exists because your boss has essentially abdicated his role as manager in order to work on his own projects, try to pick up the slack and fill the vacuum yourself. Often, in this case, the boss is valued for his technical or specialized expertise and has been promoted into management for this reason. If so, he will often welcome someone taking over the management role.

➲ *Makes impulsive or bad decisions.* One strategy here might be to help your boss make better decisions by providing additional information to steer him in the right direction when you know a decision on something is pending. Or, if you can't do anything about a bad decision, perhaps practice the art of calm detachment so you are more relaxed in facing the inevitable problems that result when the fallout from the bad decision hits the rocks of reality.

➲ *Indecisive.* As in the case of the weak and wishy-washy boss, you might try filling in to help your boss decide. In some cases, you may want to make the everyday decisions when your boss seems unwilling or unable to do so. Alternatively, get comfortable with the state of affairs and recognize that things will keep going along as they are for awhile, since not making a decision generally means maintaining the status quo.

➲ *Too nosy and invasive.* If you feel your boss is invading your personal privacy, one approach is to have a frank but polite discussion with him where you lay out the boundaries to keep your personal life out of the office. If that approach doesn't work because of your boss's insensitivity, try putting up walls to keep your boss out. For example, don't mention your private life in the office, and if your boss brings up the subject, give answers with little information. If your boss calls you at home at inappropriate times and an initial request to stop doesn't work, try screening your calls through an answering service or have another family member answer the phones and take a message. Then, unless there is a real emergency, have them inform your boss that you aren't available to take or return the call.

➲ *Yells, screams, and is rude and insulting.* You generally can't do much to stop the yelling and screaming if your boss is in an emotional state. The best response is to simply listen to let the steam boil over, and perhaps respond from time to time to show you understand what is making the boss mad. This is the sort of approach to use in any conflict situation where one party is upset, since you first have to get the emotions under control before you can deal with the problem. Then, when your boss is calmer, try to have a conversation about what made him upset so you can deal with that problem and stop the upset that led to the yelling and screaming. Alternatively, try to distance yourself and find a graceful reason not to listen to the boss's tirade, or tune him out altogether so what he says doesn't bother you. As for a boss who makes rude and insulting remarks, find a time when you can discuss the statements that bother you. If these are just occasional comments, perhaps you should just let them go, unless they are seriously offensive. In a case where the boss's remarks rise to the level of sexual harassment or racist remarks, you might want to report the incident to the boss's supervisor, to the human resources department, or—if the boss is the owner—to an appropriate outside regulatory agency.

➲ *Engages in sexual activity in the office by making unwanted sexual advances or is in a sexual relationship with another employee.* Here some key considerations include how long the activity has been going on, how aggressively the boss has been making unwanted advances, and whether this activity is disrupting the office. Also, consider if you and other employees feel the boss has been treating others unfairly by showing favoritism to an employee with whom he has a sexual relationship. For example, if the boss has been hitting on you, a good first step is to speak out and state firmly, but politely, one or more reasons that you don't want your boss making these advances. Then, if that doesn't work, you can try other measures, such as threatening to report the boss to a supervisor or to his wife. Meanwhile, continue to decline any advances and try to stay out of your boss's way so you are not caught in an intimate one-on-one situation. If your boss is involved in sexual activities with others, perhaps you should let him know that his effort to be discreet hasn't worked, that everyone knows, and that the affair is undermining morale and productivity. Perhaps seeing the company's bottom line threatened, the boss will work on being more discreet, or even stop the affair. This approach works better when a whole group confronts the boss. That way, he not only knows that everyone knows, but he knows that everyone takes this situation seriously, and it's not just you trying to share the feelings for a group.

➲ *Involved in criminal activities and asking employees to cover up or participate in these activities.* Here you want to avoid being sucked into any criminal activities or cover-ups, and the safest course may be to leave. If you stay on the job where you have knowledge that criminal activity is taking place, even if you don't actively engage in a cover-up, you might be considered complicit in the crime. As for confronting your boss about what you have discovered, that could have unpleasant repercussions, especially if this is a serious crime. So it is often better to quietly leave, not indicating your real reasons for departing, and hope for a good recommendation to take with you in your job search.

⮞ *Can't be trusted because he lies or makes promises and doesn't keep them.* You might try to have a conversation with your boss to get firm commitments on seemingly glib promises, or you might ask for clarifications when there seem to be contradictions in what a boss says at different times. By politely showing you are aware of insincere promises or false claims, you can give your boss the message that you won't be taken in and you would appreciate knowing the truth, even if it's bad news, such as a downturn in business or impending layoffs. Alternatively, if your boss makes an apparent promise, such as for a future promotion or raise, ask for a written confirmation or send a memo indicating what you understand the promise to be. Sometimes you may think the boss has made a promise when it actually is a conditional "if" statement; if something X occurs, then your boss will do Y. Similarly, if you think your boss may be lying about something important, write it down. If the lack of trust is serious enough, think about leaving (hopefully with a good recommendation) or using your written documents to support your story when you call on the union or a lawyer to represent you to get what you were promised.

⮞ *Unfair, in playing office favorites or not giving proper recognition or credit.* Office politics and rewarding favorites may be a way of life. You may be able to swing the pendulum in your favor by doing what your boss likes, thus turning *you* into one of his favorites, too. For example, take the initiative in offering to help on a project. Notice what your boss doesn't like, such as being late to a meeting, and refrain from doing it in the future, or find ways to use your social skills to get into your boss's good graces. If you aren't getting the appropriate credit, try speaking up to let your boss know of your contribution, since maybe he isn't aware of it. Or, if your boss is consciously taking the credit, understand the politics of giving credit in your workplace. In some working environments, it's par for the course for the boss to get the credit for the performance, no matter who does it. In a university research lab, for example, the professor puts his name on the paper describing the results, and the graduate students and interns know in advance not to expect any credit. At most, they may receive a brief mention. If you are in an office where your boss isn't appropriately giving credit whereas other managers are, maybe you can find a way to let others know, such as casually mentioning "the project I worked on" in a meeting. The subtle comment will put your boss on notice that you are claiming credit for your work, and he may give credit in the future. However, if this lack of recognition continues to be a problem, you may have to learn to live with not getting the credit while you are there. Try for a good recommendation when you later decide to move on, and include these projects on your resume.

In short, think of these different situations and strategies as starting points for what may work with various kinds of bad bosses. Then, adapt your strategy based on other factors that may come into play in your particular circumstances.

Other Factors to Consider and Questions to Ask

Some other factors to consider and questions to ask in helping you decide what to do in your particular situation are:

➲ *Why is my boss acting this way? Is it his personal style? Does he act this way with everyone, or just with me? Is there something I might be doing that is leading my boss to act this way, such as my acting unsure that I can accomplish a task he wants me to do?* Your answers will reveal whether this is an individual issue to deal with yourself or something that affects the whole office, and whether this is a situation where you might be able to change how to do the work in order to improve your relationship with the boss.

➲ *What is my own goal or desired outcome in this situation? Do I want to change the situation? Would I like to make the best of a bad situation? Do I want to get out and get a good recommendation? How would I prioritize these different goals and outcomes?* By knowing what you want, you are in a better position to decide which strategy to attempt first.

⊃ *How do others in the office who might be similarly affected feel about the boss? What are their goals for change? Would they like me to speak for them? Can I involve others, so we plan to deal with the boss as a group?* By knowing who else is involved, and how they perceive the situation and would like to deal with it, you can better strategize whether to approach your boss individually or as part of a group, and how to best make this approach.

⊃ *How does my boss prefer to deal with conflicts and problems in the office? Is he open to communicating about them? If so, what is generally the most common or effective way to do this? Having a one-on-one meeting, having a phone conversation, sending a memo, or writing an e-mail? Alternatively, does he generally prefer to avoid dealing with problems directly? Would he like employees to handle these issues themselves?* Once you know your boss's preferred communication style and receptivity to hearing about any problems, you can employ the most compatible approach.

⊃ *What's my own personality style? What kind of approach am I most comfortable with? Would I rather have a meeting, phone conversation, or send a memo or e-mail?* While it's a good idea to put your boss's personality style first, if you feel uneasy, fall back on the approach that is most comfortable for you. For instance, if you are shy and feel uncomfortable speaking up to an outgoing boss, find another approach that will work better for you, such as writing everything down in a diplomatically phrased letter.

⊃ *How important is this issue? Does this need attention right away, say, because it is undermining office morale and productivity? Or am I the only one who is bothered and if so, is there a better time to raise the subject?* The consideration here is the timing. If the issue is very important, it may be best to act quickly. If not, perhaps waiting would be better, since that will give you, your boss, and anyone else involved in the problem a cooling-off period during which you can plan and strategize what's best to do.

⊃ *How likely am I to succeed? How likely is it that my boss is going to change?* The consideration here is whether to bring up the issue at all. If you feel your boss is set in his ways and has the power to continue what he is doing, due to personal power or office politics, maybe it's best to go along to get along for the time being. It may be more advantageous to endure until you have an opportunity for a favorable result, such as transferring to another department or finding a new job in another company.

➲ *What's the political environment like? How powerful is my boss? How much power or influence do I have in my position? How valuable is the work I am doing, and how easily can I be replaced? What kind of support does he have from others, or is he the company owner? Are there any outside factors that might affect my boss, such as a spouse, community influence, or government regulations?* By asking these questions, you cannot only consider the likelihood of your success in seeking change, but can come up with some strategic ways to do achieve it. For example, under some circumstances, you might gain success by going to your boss's boss or spouse to help you make desired changes; in other cases, that move could get you fired for insubordination. Or if your boss is doing something that's clearly illegal or criminal, you might go to the authorities with your complaints.

➲ *How would I feel if this situation continues as is? How important is it to me that this situation changes, or can I live with this problem for now?* The answers to this question can help you think about whether you really want to press for some change right now. Even if the issue is a very important one to you, maybe you would rather wait and accept it for now, rather than rocking the boat. For example, if the company is likely to experience downsizing in the future and your boss may not be there in a month or two, maybe you'd be better off doing nothing about the problem until the upcoming restructuring shakes out.

➲ *What is the risk of bringing up the problem with my boss or others in the company? What is the worst-case scenario?* These questions will help you assess the downside risk of taking some action so you can determine whether you are willing to take the risk or not.

➲ *Are there any communication problems or flawed assumptions that may be at the root of the problem?* Sometimes difficulties with a boss develop because he isn't a good communicator and doesn't give clear instructions or listen carefully to what you say. Or maybe you aren't communicating sufficiently with your boss, so he doesn't know what you are doing, and may supervise, micromanage, and use more controls than otherwise necessary. Improving a relationship or solving a problem may thus depend on clarifying your communications, or correcting or smoothing over any misunderstandings that occur when communications are unclear.

In addition, wrong assumptions may lead to problems because people don't have the facts or jump to conclusions based on faulty assumptions. A good example is when your boss doesn't trust you to do something because he has had a bad experience with a previous employee and thinks you may be the same. Another possibility may be that you think your boss doesn't trust you because of the close monitoring, whereas your boss is thinking this careful supervision is a way to be more helpful and give you better feedback. Thus, a key to reducing such problems is to check whether your conclusions or assumptions are correct, or to recognize that someone else is acting on faulty conclusions or assumptions and correcting this error.

Depending on the situation, you may have other questions, too. The basic idea is that, in deciding how to handle your situation, you should raise a number of relevant questions to help you assess a number of factors including what is really going on, how strongly you feel about it, what alternatives you have for responding, the likelihood for success of each option, and the downside risk if you act—or don't. Then, you can better decide what action to take.

Unfortunately, popular advice columns to the contrary, there is often no clear-cut or easy solution for what to do, if anything, about a bad boss. The reason that the easy directives often don't work is because the best option usually depends on multiple factors that include, among other things, you, your boss, the role of other employees and supervisors, the culture of your industry, and the particulars of the situation. So you need to know what's really going on before you can best decide what to do.

Some Techniques for Making a Good Decision

Making a good decision starts with understanding what's going on, a process you can perform rationally or by using your intuition. Then, with these insights, you can draw on a repertoire of tools and techniques to help you determine what to do. I've described these techniques in more detail in my previous book, *A Survival Guide to Working with Humans*. Here's a brief recap of what tools you might use.

- ⮑ *Visualize possible options and outcomes.* You can use visualization to imagine different scenarios for dealing with your boss and the possible outcomes. Then, choose the outcome that seems your best alternative at the time. To use visualization or mental imaging, first get very relaxed and comfortable. Find a quiet place to do this. Next, imagine you are watching film in your mind's eye and that you are the movie director. Try different responses and let the scene play out, without trying to direct it yourself.

- ⮑ *Use visualization for goal setting, preparation, and planning.* Say you have already come up with an alternative, such as having a frank conversation with your boss. Then, with this chosen outcome in mind, think about what steps you will need to take to get there, such as how to set up the meeting and what to say. One way to visualize these steps is to see a path to your goal with a series of stops or signposts along the way. Then, as you go to each stop, visualize what you will do at that location.

  You can combine any of these steps with affirmations, self-talk, or other types of reinforcements to help you feel more powerful and confident when you put these actions into practice. For instance, suppose you want to talk to your boss about what you perceive as unfair treatment and a lack of appropriate recognition and credit. You might see yourself going into his office and practicing what you will say in your mind. Then, you might conclude the visualization by telling yourself, "I will get more credit" or "My boss will give me the credit I'm asking for."

- ⮑ *Weigh the positives and negatives to do what's practical.* Another way to decide what to do and how is to make a positive/negative, cost/benefit, or pro/con analysis. You can do this systematically by listing the pros and cons for each alternative you are considering to deal with your boss, using weighted ratings to compare and contrast them. Or you can make this assessment using a more intuitive, instant analysis. In this case, list each alternative, get very relaxed, and let your unconscious give you a rating from 1 (low) to 10 (high) on how practical each action would be.

Use the E-R-I model for resolving conflicts with your boss. If you are having a conflict with your boss or are dealing with an especially angry or emotional boss, the "E-R-I" Model (where "E-R-I" stands for the Emotions, Reasons, and Intuition) can help. The first step is to get the negative *emotions* out of the way. Do this by either getting your own emotions under control or by listening calmly while your boss vents to blow off steam, thereby detaching yourself from the situation so you don't get upset or try to yell back and escalate the situation. In step two, you use your deductive *reasoning* to understand the reasons for the conflict by thinking about the different factors that contribute to it, from your boss's personality to workplace conditions. Additionally, use your reason to understand the different resolution styles you might use to resolve a conflict. In dealing with a boss, you probably don't want to use the first conflict resolution method, which is *confrontation,* where you exercise your power to seek what you want, since you are, by definition, in a low-power position. Openly confronting the boss can get you fired for insubordination and being considered a difficult employee. But the other four conflict resolution methods might work, and you can use visualization to think about which approach to use to decide what to do. These are:

1. *Collaboration,* where you and other parties to the conflict take time to consider the different issues and resolve them together.
2. *Compromise,* where you each give a little.
3. *Accommodation,* where you give in to what someone else wants, because they have more power or the issue isn't that important to you.
4. *Avoidance,* where you choose not to deal with the conflict by seeking to leave, not thinking about it, or delaying any action.

Finally, in step three, as you think about applying these different conflict styles, use your *intuition* to brainstorm different alternatives and choose among them.

Putting It All Together

To sum up, a good way to approach any problem with a bad boss is by first carefully examining the situation to discover what's going on. Is the problem due to your boss's usual personality or style, or is something triggering the problem from time to time, and if so, what?

Then, consider the overall situation in your workplace, such as whether this problem affects just you or is more general throughout the workplace, your own power, the importance of your work, and any other factors that contribute to the current difficulties with your boss. Also, consider your ideal goal. What you would really like to do to resolve the situation? What is the likelihood of this happening, and what other possible scenarios exist for achieving a positive outcome? Factor in the worst-case scenario, too, when you weigh your options. Finally, look at the various techniques you might use to help you choose and implement a particular approach.

The stories in this book are examples of how others have dealt with these difficult boss situations, and their experiences may help you figure out what to do in your own situation. In future books, I'll feature other workplace stories, from dealing with bad bosses to dealing with difficult coworkers, employees, customers, and problem situations in general. I invite you to send in your own stories to be used in future books, and I will seek to help you resolve your problem in a personal response.

To summarize the major techniques to apply in dealing with bad bosses, here they are one last time in brief. Feel free to add your own thoughts as well.

The Major Techniques for Dealing with Bad Bosses

The major techniques are:
1. Assess the different factors contributing to the situation.
2. Visualize possible options and outcomes.
3. Use visualization for goal setting, preparation, and planning.
4. Decide what's practical by weighing the positives and negatives.
5. Use the E-R-I Model for resolving conflicts or dealing with a bad boss who's angry or upset.
6. Clear up communication problems by asking questions for clarification or providing a more detailed explanation yourself.

(continues)

> 7. **Check out conclusions and assumptions by getting the facts.**
> 8. **Other?**

Today's Take-Aways:

☑ Think about how the general principles might apply in your situation, but keep in mind that every bad-boss situation is different.

☑ Use the examples of what others have done in dealing with their own bad bosses to consider possible approaches for your own case, then adapt those solutions to your situation.

☑ Begin by thinking about the situation so you really understand what's going on; then consider the various factors that may impact on the problem and what you might do to solve it.

☑ Once you understand what to do, think of the options you might use, and consider the pros and cons of different approaches.

☑ Use visualization or mental imaging to help determine possible options and outcomes; then choose which alternative would be best for you.

Index

About the Author

Gini Graham Scott, Ph.D., J.D., is a nationally known writer, consultant, speaker, and seminar/workshop leader, specializing in business and work relationships, and professional and personal development. She is founder and director of Changemakers and Creative Communications & Research, and has published more than forty books on diverse subjects. Her previous books on business relationships and professional development include: *A Survival Guide to Working with Humans, Work with Me! Resolving Everyday Conflict in Your Organization,* and *Resolving Conflict.* Her books on professional and personal development include *The Empowered Mind: How to Harness the Creative Force Within You* and *Mind Power: Picture Your Way to Success.*

Gini Scott has received national media exposure for her books, including appearances on *Good Morning America!, Oprah, Montel Williams,* CNN, and *The O'Reilly Factor.* She additionally has written a dozen screenplays, several signed to agents or optioned by producers, and has been a game designer, with more than two dozen games on the market with major game companies, including Hasbro, Pressman, and Mag-Nif.

She has taught classes at several colleges, including California State University at Hayward, Notre Dame de Namur University, and the Investigative Career Program in San Francisco. She received a Ph.D. in Sociology from the University of California in Berkeley, a J.D. from the University of San Francisco Law School, an M.A. in

Anthropology, Mass Communications, and Organizational, Consumer, and Audience Behavior from Cal State University, East Bay.

She is also the founder and director of PublishersAndAgents.net, which connects writers with publishers, literary agents, film producers, and film agents. The three-year-old service has served more than 500 clients, and has been written up in the *Wall Street Journal* and other publications.

For more information, you can visit www.ginigrahamscott.com, which includes a video of media clips and speaking engagements, and www.giniscott.com, which features her books. Or call or write to Gini Scott at her company:

Changemakers
6114 La Salle, #358
Oakland, CA 94611
(510) 339-1625
changemakers@pacbell.net